New Directions for Student Services

Elizabeth J. Whitt
EDITOR-IN-CHIEF

John H. Schuh
ASSOCIATE EDITOR

Stepping Up to Stepping Out: Helping Students Prepare for Life after College

George S. McClellan
and Jill Parker
EDITORS

Number 138 • Summer 2012
Jossey-Bass
San Francisco

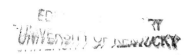
Stepping Up to Stepping Out: Helping Students Prepare for Life after College
George S. McClellan and Jill Parker (eds.)
New Directions for Student Services, no. 138
Elizabeth J. Whitt, Editor-in-Chief
John H. Schuh, Associate Editor

New Directions for Student Services (ISSN 0164-7970, e-ISSN 1536-0695) is part of The Jossey-Bass Higher and Adult Education Series and is published quarterly by Wiley Subscription Services, Inc., A Wiley Company, at Jossey-Bass, One Montgomery Street, Suite 1200, San Francisco, CA 94104-4594. Periodicals Postage Paid at San Francisco, California, and at additional mailing offices. POSTMASTER: Send address changes to New Directions for Student Services, Jossey-Bass, One Montgomery Street, Suite 1200, San Francisco, CA 94104-4594.

New Directions for Student Services is indexed in CIJE: Current Index to Journals in Education (ERIC), Contents Pages in Education (T&F), Current Abstracts (EBSCO), Education Index/Abstracts (H.W. Wilson), Educational Research Abstracts Online (T&F), ERIC Database (Education Resources Information Center), and Higher Education Abstracts (Claremont Graduate University).

Microfilm copies of issues and articles are available in 16mm and 35mm, as well as microfiche in 105mm, through University Microfilms Inc., 300 North Zeeb Road, Ann Arbor, Michigan 48106-1346.

Subscriptions cost $89.00 for individuals and $275.00 for institutions, agencies, and libraries in the United States.

Editorial correspondence should be sent to the Editor-in-Chief, Elizabeth J. Whitt, N473 Lindquist Center, The University of Iowa, Iowa City, IA 52242.

www.josseybass.com

CONTENTS

Editors' Notes

One constant in the course of the history of higher education in the United States is that its goal has always been to prepare students for full and meaningful lives after college. However, both the vision of what form that preparation should take and the composition of the student body have been in a continuous state of change throughout that same span of time. Our purpose in presenting this monograph is to offer a discussion of contemporary practices in preparing students for life after college, while taking note of the history and also offering some thoughts on the future.

The New Directions in Student Services series comprises texts that are intended to be sourcebooks—that is, they are meant to be practical, timely, and relatively brief. Managing a discussion on preparing students for after-college life within the series' framework requires that we make some decisions regarding both the content and the organization of the chapters being solicited from our authors.

The first choice we addressed was establishing the scope of content for the monograph. Life after college is a fairly broad landscape. Narrowing the scope of the discussion to focus on preparing students for particular types of transitions seemed reasonable, in order to assure that the monograph would prove significantly helpful to our readers. Recognizing that such narrowing would also minimize discussion of other forms of transition, we made two choices related to scope. First, we decided to limit the discussion to life after undergraduate education. This choice was driven by the practical consideration of the greater number of students involved in these transitions and the corresponding number of student affairs professionals and others involved in helping these students. Preparing graduate and professional students for life after college is another important and interesting opportunity for student affairs professionals, and we hope to see discussions on this topic in future articles, chapters, monographs, and books.

Having chosen to address undergraduate education, our second choice was to focus the discussion on three particular activities of life after college: transition from one form of education (two-year or four-year) to the next (four-year or graduate and professional school), transition from education to workforce, and transition from education to military service. Here again our thinking was guided by practical considerations regarding the numbers of students who are engaged in each of these three transitions. Discussion of the transition from education to a period of public service, or to a period of personal exploration and reflection, or to a period of building a family would all be welcome additions to the literature of student affairs. Another welcome addition to the literature, albeit a challenging one to organize given its considerable scope, would be a monograph (or book)

New Directions for Student Services, no. 138, Summer 2012 © Wiley Periodicals, Inc.
Published online in Wiley Online Library (wileyonlinelibrary.com) • DOI: 10.1002/ss.20001

focused on helping students to develop life skills related to financial literacy and health, including money management, handling of contracts (employment, leases, loans, etc.), and insurance in various forms.

Having determined what content we wanted authors to address, we needed to make choices related to organizing the material, and we decided upon a fairly traditional path. We would open with a presentation of history and contemporary context of practice followed by a discussion of theories applicable to practice. Next, we would move to programmatic approaches to preparing students for after-college life with a chapter offering an overview and a chapter offering case studies. Switching to curricular approaches, again we would offer an overview chapter and a case study chapter. The monograph would conclude with a look toward the future that draws upon the information shared in its chapters.

Consideration of all these choices prompted an important insight. For the purposes of efficiency, we adopted a set of common definitions and distinctions in designing the monograph. We chose to discuss transitions from undergraduate education to further education, or to workforce, or to military service. We distinguished between programmatic and curricular (or, put another way, student affairs and academic affairs) approaches as an organizing principle. The reality of our work with students, however, is far richer than the simple one-dimensional constructs that we use to frame our consideration of that work. Our students are engaged in various forms of education simultaneously. They may be taking high school and college courses or undergraduate- and graduate-level courses. Many of them are already working, and some of these are already working in their chosen career. A course, series of courses, or a degree is not their gateway transition; it is more of an evolutionary step. With the state of global affairs and the demands on our military services, students today may not have the luxury of moving through their education and then into service. They are serving or training for service while in school and moving back and forth between being more a soldier than a student and vice versa. Finally, both of us fully believe that the shared focus of students, staff, and faculty ought to be on student learning and development. When that is the case, the traditional artificial distinction between programmatic and curricular approaches is far less relevant. So, while we stand by our choices regarding managing the monograph for better or for worse, we need to be clear and explicit about those choices and about their limitations.

We also want to be thorough in thanking all of those who have helped bring this monograph to fruition. First and foremost, thanks to the authors who answered our call to contribute. Your thoughtfulness and diligence are greatly appreciated! In thanking the authors, we recognize and appreciate the contribution made by Joel Driver and Brian Montalvo to the development of Chapter Three. Similarly, we are happy to acknowledge the assistance offered by Karen Obringer in finalizing the manuscript. We also thank John Schuh and Liz Whitt for inviting us to serve as editors for this monograph. The work the two of you have accomplished as editors for the New Directions in Student Services series is a remarkable gift to our profession. We have enjoyed the opportunity to learn through the experience of working on this project, including learning to be careful when John starts looking around for volunteers.

George McClellan thanks Peggy Barr for her continued friendship and mentorship, his colleagues at IPFW for their work in support of student success and their encouragement of his scholarly endeavors, and Jill Parker for serving as coeditor. Her hard work, sharp mind, keen eye, steady focus, and easy wit mark her promise as a writer and editor moving forward.

Jill Parker thanks her parents for their support, her Front Range Community College colleagues for their tireless work in serving students, and George McClellan for his guidance, patience, and mentorship. The opportunity to assist with editing this monograph has been an incredible learning experience, and George's willingness to teach the fine art of editing, at which he excels, is greatly appreciated. Jill would also like to thank her friend and colleague, Joel Driver, for his friendship, encouragement, and support. Joel, an initial contributor to this monograph, lost his long-fought battle with cancer in January 2012, and he is dearly missed by his family, friends, and colleagues.

We hope you will find this monograph helpful in providing information about assisting students in preparing for life after college and useful in stimulating ideas for the ways in which you can enhance programs and courses on your campus in this area. Thank you.

George S. McClellan
Jill Parker
Editors

GEORGE S. MCCLELLAN is vice chancellor for Student Affairs at Indiana University–Purdue University Fort Wayne and coeditor of the Handbook for Student Affairs Administration (3rd ed.). *Prior to his current position, McClellan served in a variety of student affairs roles at Northwestern University, University of Arizona, and Dickinson State University.*

JILL PARKER is director of Advising, Career, and Retention Services at Front Range Community College–Larimer Campus. She was formerly the Director of Career Services at Indiana University–Purdue University Fort Wayne.

NEW DIRECTIONS FOR STUDENT SERVICES • DOI: 10.1002/ss

1

This chapter addresses the context in which student affairs professionals, faculty, and other mentors prepare students for after-college life.

Preparing Students for After-College Life: The Context

Kelli K. Smith

What role do colleges and universities play in preparing students for life after college? Much like parents who continually balance *caring* for their child versus *carrying* their child, colleges and universities must define their role in educating students in a way that will assist them not only during their time as students, but for the long term as well. Historical context informs the work of student affairs professionals and others in higher education in striking the right balance in helping prepare students for life after college, but significant new pressures face students, their mentors, and educational institutions today.

This chapter discusses the contexts that shape the work of student affairs professionals and their colleagues in helping students prepare for life after their undergraduate experience. That discussion begins with a brief review of the historical context and then moves to a lengthier review of the contemporary context.

Historical Context

Colleges in the United States have always prepared students for life after college, but the form of that preparation has changed over time. To some degree, the extent to which colleges and universities in the United States are expected to prepare students for life after college has roots in the doctrine of *in loco parentis*, a Latin phrase that means "in the place of a parent." The roots of *in loco parentis* extend beyond the American educational system, and the progression of the concept over time relates to the context in which student affairs professionals, faculty, and others prepare students for after-college life.

NEW DIRECTIONS FOR STUDENT SERVICES, no. 138, Summer 2012 © Wiley Periodicals, Inc.
Published online in Wiley Online Library (wileyonlinelibrary.com) • DOI: 10.1002/ss.20002

Early in the history of the United States, colleges primarily followed the model of the English residential university system in which faculty were expected to attend to the intellectual, moral, social, and spiritual development of young students. The work of the faculty was focused on the formal curriculum and matters pertaining to it. This traditional model was in place from the establishment of Harvard in 1636 to approximately the last third of the nineteenth century, and it was quite different from the more laissez-faire treatment of students within German universities (Komives and Woodward, 2003). Later, however, faculty at leading institutions within the United States became more focused on research and scholarship and less engaged with the lives of students. This shift led to students creating a rich extracurricular life on their own. Responsibilities for regulating, disciplining, and advising students transferred from faculty to staff, and the earliest version of what is now known as student affairs emerged (Komives and Woodward, 2003). The holistic approach to educating students emerged and became predominant in higher education. At the same time, there was greater recognition of students' responsibilities for shaping their own learning and experiences both in and out of the classroom.

Another important historical development in American higher education relates to the relationship between college and careers. In the earliest days, students who attended college came largely from families of means and were not attending college to prepare for a career. The presumption was that these students would have roles as owners of businesses, leaders of the community, or respected members of the clergy. They attended college to assure their readiness as leading members of society. Over time, specialization and professionalization increased, which drove the need for more educated individuals in the workforce. The most elite institutions continued their emphasis on preparing leaders, while other institutions sprang up to serve the needs of the broader public and booming economy. These new institutions grew to be fairly explicit in linking their curricular and cocurricular offerings to career development. Indeed, even the elite institutions have moved in this direction.

Contemporary Context

The historical development of higher education and student affairs in the United States shapes contemporary practice in two important ways. First, it is generally recognized that faculty, student affairs professionals and other staff, and students share responsibility for the student experience and student success in higher education. Second, a holistic perspective informs the vision of what that experience should be and how success is defined.

This section of the chapter addresses several current issues and trends that, informed by historical developments, have an impact on contemporary practice. These issues and trends include: increased expectations regarding accountability, renewed focus on learning, evolving student demographics, changing and challenging economic conditions, and building relationships in the face of disappearing boundaries and borders.

Accountability. Students, their families, legislatures, philanthropists, and the public-at-large have always had high expectations of higher education. In an era of rising costs, increasing options, and challenging economic horizons, those expectations have taken on the more concrete form of demands for accountability for their investments. The call for greater accountability manifests itself in a variety of ways related to the work of preparing students for life after college.

Family Involvement. Given that both students and their family members identify career goals as the number-one reason for attending college, it is not surprising to find that family members are increasingly involved in decisions regarding the education experiences of students. Parents, grandparents, guardians, and spouses or partners expect to be a part, and at times a significant part, of students' choices regarding college from beginning to the end, a phenomenon that is sometimes referred to as helicopter parenting (Young, 2003), and which some feel has reached a fevered pitch over the past several years (Golden, 2010).

While some in higher education decry what they perceive as the over-involvement of family, others view family as partners. This development has led colleges and universities to begin marketing to both prospective students *and* their families, and it is not too surprising when family members want to meet with a career counselor alongside their student trying to decide upon a major.

Clearly, the nature of the university-student-family relationship has changed in recent years. This new relationship comes with both challenges and opportunities, such as increased access to staff and faculty, higher expectations for job placement, and a desire for value-added services and programs.

Another manifestation of heightened expectations of accountability is evidenced by recent regulatory activity regarding the gainful employment provisions included in Title IV of the Higher Education Act (United States Department of Education, 2011). While this activity has been centered on for-profit colleges, there are those in the not-for-profit sector of higher education who are concerned that their work may come under additional scrutiny as well (Epstein, 2010).

Learning. While *in loco parentis* has not disappeared completely as a guiding construct in higher education, universities in the United States have shifted their primary framework for working with students to learning and development (Bickel and Lake, 1999). Within this context, the student affairs profession has evolved to using more of an educational model than a paternalistic one.

Intentionally creating conditions that enhance student learning and development, as advocated in the seminal publication *The Student Learning*

NEW DIRECTIONS FOR STUDENT SERVICES • DOI: 10.1002/ss

Imperative: Implications for Student Affairs (American College Personnel Association, 1996), is critical for today's uncertain society. College graduates face a harsh economic climate, a plethora of new career choices, technologies and modes of communication that change daily, an enormously divided political landscape, and social forces that have altered family roles. Educating students on how to prepare for life after college, rather than coddling or controlling them, sets them up for success.

Student Demographics. To fully meet the duty of educating students and preparing them for life after college, it is essential for student affairs professionals to be familiar with the profile of the students they serve. National trends of student characteristics such as age, socioeconomic status, gender, and race have been well documented. However, it is important to examine such factors across institutional types and to be well informed regarding local demographics. Institutions of higher education differ widely, as do the student bodies they serve. For example, a small private institution in a rural area, an urban community college, and a large land-grant public institution would each, quite likely, produce unique student profiles. In addition to recognizing and understanding the profile of the student body they serve within their own institutional setting, student affairs professionals should also be familiar with general student characteristics that change over time (Komives and Woodard, 2003). Information on trends in student characteristics is readily available, yet "sadly, student affairs staff do not always take full advantage of such information" (p. 405).

While individual institutions each have their own unique student profile, there are several national trends that are particularly salient with regard to preparing students for life after college. First, some argue that there is a constant need for direction and a lack of leadership and independence in the current generation of college students (Alsop, 2008). Whether real or not, the perception of the employers Alsop interviewed was that the current generation of college graduates lacked these characteristics. Another study of employers suggested students are prepared for their first job but not higher-level positions that require critical thinking, the ability to direct themselves, and management of uncertainty (Peter D. Hart Research Associates, 2008).

Second, students today are highly confident and individualistic. Twenge (2006) argues that, in addition to these characteristics, today's students possess self-perceptions regarding their abilities that are not congruent with reality. The author contends that while it might seem intuitive that the more individualistic one is, the more independent one would be, the reality is that the emphasis on uniqueness has led the current generation of college students to have an element of entitlement. Rather than having the ability to persevere, they tend to expect others to figure things out for them. There are, undoubtedly, implications for their lives after graduation here. Student affairs professionals are in prime positions to assist students in this regard. For example, opportunities to help students develop a sense of agency and self-efficacy are plentiful in collegiate programs and services. Developing programs and services to foster realistic expectations, adaptability, and resiliency (Luthans, 2002) in college seniors would likely assist college graduates later in life (Murphy, Blustein, Bohling, and Platt, 2010).

Economic Conditions. Today's college graduates are entering into the most challenging economic environment in decades (Yousuf, 2009), though there are some signs that the job market is up a bit from its near-record lows of 2008–2010 (Stafford, 2011). It is not surprising given the condition of the economy that the debate regarding whether or not college is worth the investment has resurfaced (Carnevale, 2011; Vedder, 2011). However academicians and policy makers measure the relative merits of personal investment in higher education, it is clear that students (and their families) continue to see completing a college degree as an important pathway to building their future.

Though it is difficult to estimate how often individuals change both jobs and careers (United States Bureau of Labor Statistics, 2010b), the vast majority of today's students can certainly expect to have several changes in jobs and careers throughout their lifetime. Also, the rising rate at which new career fields emerge has skyrocketed. In 2010, the Bureau of Labor Statistics (BLS) began to develop and implement the collection of new data on green jobs (United States Bureau of Labor Statistics, 2010a). The impact of globalization and technology has also spurred the creation of new career paths. Therefore, *teaching* students how to choose a career or search for a job, for example, is critical. Additionally, it is imperative that students leave college fully prepared with the skill sets necessary to be successful in whatever career they choose.

Many students choose to attend graduate or professional school either immediately after their undergraduate education or several years down the road, and that is even more the case in the face of uncertain opportunities and rising expectations on the part of employers with regard to minimum requirements for positions. There is the question of whose responsibility it is to prepare students for that chapter of their lives. Is it their faculty advisor? A McNair program advisor? The career center? The student's responsibility on their own? Others? Much like other areas, cross-campus collaborations are needed to help students reach their full potential of preparedness for graduate education. Students need a solid grounding in research and writing during their undergraduate experience, areas that are worthy of concentrated effort even for students unsure of their postbaccalaureate plans, but especially when considering graduate or professional school. This may take the form of sponsored summer research appointments through the National Science Foundation at another university, or research on campus with a faculty member in their department of study. Such experiences, along with other activities outside of course assignments and projects, can be very helpful in informing decisions about graduate studies, fields of possible specialization, and careers. Advising and mentoring on the application process is also needed for students contemplating graduate education.

Building Relationships, Disappearing Borders. In the face of difficult economic times, it is arguably more important than ever that student affairs professionals engage in partnerships with colleagues from across campus and throughout the community to create programs and services that fully prepare students for postgraduate life. The 2010 joint ACPA and NASPA task force report *Envisioning the Future of Student Affairs* placed further emphasis on collaborative partnerships:

> In the new view of student affairs work, on-campus partnerships continue to be essential and challenging. Breaking down internal silos, while critical, is not enough. The mobility of students and the diversity of their experiences require a rethinking of the nature of student affairs collaborations. (American College Personnel Association and National Association of Student Personnel Administrators, 2010)

It is particularly important for colleagues in academic affairs and student affairs to collaborate creatively in enhancing student learning (Smith, 2005). There is research to support the idea that campus communities characterized by such collaborations offer an environment that promotes student success (Kezar, Hirsch, and Burack, 2002; Kinzie and Kuh, 2004; Schuh and Whitt, 1999).

The joint ACPA and NASPA task force also called for an expanded view of partnerships by encouraging colleges and universities to collaborate with entities beyond campus borders, such as private industry and community agencies, in addition to those outside local, state, and national boundaries. There are many programs that assist in preparing students for their later years that require such collaborations. U.S. students are studying abroad in unprecedented numbers. Service-learning programs offer students experiences locally, nationally, and internationally. Internships can occur in a student's hometown or in Tokyo, Japan. Implications for preparing students for life in a globalized society necessitate an expanded view of collaborative partnerships.

Conclusion

Henscheid (2008) identifies both academic experiences and cocurricular programs as important elements in helping prepare students for success after college. Further, Henscheid suggests that "attention also needs to be focused on making the connections between intellectual, personal, and social outcomes more explicit" (2008, p. 25). The authors of another study examining the transition of recent college graduates suggest additional ways in which institutions can prepare college seniors for the transition to careers. Programming for groups of students about to graduate to increase awareness of the common challenges and potential disappointments they might encounter, along with training modules to educate undergraduates about the goals of employers, could prove beneficial (Murphy et al., 2010).

What better profession is there to do this, and thus teach students how to live a fulfilling life outside the classroom, than student affairs? This chapter addresses the historical and contemporary context in which student affairs professionals and others prepare students for after-college life. Subsequent chapters discuss applicable theories and models of practice, overviews and case studies of programmatic and curricular approaches, and thoughts on the future in this area.

References

Alsop, R. *The Trophy Kids Grow Up: How the Millennial Generation Is Shaking Up the Workplace*. San Francisco: Jossey-Bass, 2008.

American College Personnel Association. *The Student Learning Imperative: Implications for Student Affairs*. Washington, DC: Author, 1996.

American College Personnel Association and National Association of Student Personnel Administrators. "Envisioning the Future of Student Affairs." Washington, DC: Authors, 2010.

Bickel, R. D., and Lake, P. F. *The Rights and Responsibilities of the Modern University*. Durham, NC: Carolina Academic Press, 1999.

Carnevale, A. "College Is Still Worth It." *Inside Higher Education*, Jan. 14, 2011. Retrieved June 29, 2011, from http://www.insidehighered.com/views/2011/01/14/carnevale_college_is_still_worth_it_for_americans.

Epstein, J. "Going Ahead with Gainful Employment." *Inside Higher Education*, Apr. 21, 2010. Retrieved June 29, 2011, from http://www.insidehighered.com/news/2010/04/21/gainful.

Golden, S. "How Anxious Parents Affect Colleges, Students' Experience." *USA Today*, June 3, 2010. Retrieved June 29, 2011, from http://www.usatoday.com/news/education/2010-06-03-IHE-anxious-parents-college03_ST_N.htm.

Henscheid, J. M. "Preparing Seniors for Life after College." *About Campus*, 13(5), 2008.

Kezar, A., Hirsch, D., and Burack, C. (Eds.) *Achieving Student Success: Collaboration between Academic and Student Affairs*. San Francisco: Jossey-Bass, 2002.

Kinzie, J., and Kuh, G. D. "Going DEEP: Learning from Campuses That Share Responsibility for Student Success." *About Campus*, 9(5), 2004.

Komives, S. R., and Woodward, D. B., Jr. (Eds.). *Student Services: A Handbook for the Profession* (4th ed.). San Francisco: Jossey-Bass, 2003.

Luthans, F. "The Need for and Meaning of Positive Organizational Behavior." *Journal of Organizational Behavior*, 23, 2002.

Murphy, K. A., Blustein, D. L, Bohling, A. J., and Platt, M. G. "The College-to-Career Transition: An Exploration of Emerging Adulthood." *Journal of Counseling and Development*, 88, 2010.

Peter D. Hart Research Associates. "How Should Colleges Assess and Improve Student Learning?" Washington, DC: Author. Retrieved June 29, 2011, from http://www.aacu.org/leap/documents/2008_Business_Leader_Poll.pdf, 2008.

Schuh, J. H., and Whitt, E. J. (eds.). *Creating Successful Partnerships between Academic and Student Affairs*. San Francisco: Jossey-Bass, 1999.

Smith, K. K. "From Coexistence to Collaboration: A Call for Partnership between Academic and Student Affairs." *Journal of Cognitive and Affective Learning*, 2(1), 2005.

Stafford, D. "Job Prospects Brighten Slightly for 2011 College Graduates." Kansas City Star, May 20, 2011. Retrieved June 29, 2011, from http://www.kansascity.com/2011/05/08/2860013/future-brightens-for-2011-graduates.html.

Twenge, J. M. *Generation Me: Why Today's Young Americans Are More Confident, Assertive, Entitled—and More Miserable Than Ever Before.* New York: Free Press, 2006.

United States Bureau of Labor Statistics, "Measuring Green Jobs." Retrieved Oct. 7, 2010, from http://www.bls.gov/green/home.htm, 2010a.

United States Bureau of Labor Statistics, "National Longitudinal Surveys." Retrieved Nov. 25, 2010, from http://www.bls.gov/nls/nlsfaqs.htm#anch41, 2010b.

United States Department of Education. "Obama Administration Announces New Steps to Protect from Ineffective Career College Programs." Retrieved June 29, 2011, from http://www.ed.gov/news/press-releases/gainful-employment-regulations.

Vedder, R. "For Many, College Isn't Worth It." *Inside Higher Education*, Jan. 20, 2011. Retrieved June 29, 2011, from http://www.insidehighered.com/views/2011/01/20/vedder_going_to_college_isn_t_a_smart_decision_for_many_young_people.

Young, J. R. (Jan. 31, 2003). "A New Take on What Today's Students Want from College." *Chronicle of Higher Education*, 49(21), A37, Jan. 31, 2003. Retrieved Oct. 21, 2010, from http://chronicle.com/article/A-New-Take-on-What-Todays/5696.

Yousuf, H. "Job Outlook for 2010 Grads: Still Stinks." Cable News Network (CNN), Nov. 18, 2009. Retrieved June 29, 2011, from http://money.cnn.com/2009/11/17/news/economy/college_graduates_jobs/index.htm.

KELLI K. SMITH *is assistant director of Career Services and an adjunct faculty member at the University of Nebraska–Lincoln.*

2

This chapter explores theories and models that can inform student affairs practitioners and faculty in preparing students for life after college.

Engaging Theories and Models to Inform Practice

Amanda Kraus

The college experience is regarded as critical for providing the context and environment for students' moral, ethical, cognitive, and identity development (Evans, Forney, Guido, Patton, and Renn, 2010; Pascarella and Terenzini, 2005), and there are a myriad of theories and models available to illuminate these processes. Ample literature and research is dedicated to understanding how theory may inform student affairs professionals and faculty in their work with college students. Theories offer insights, tools, and strategies useful in supporting students in their initial transition to college—involvement, integration, persistence, and ultimately their retention and graduation. However, while graduation is the closing marker for one phase of life, it is the opening ceremony for another. Student affairs professionals and others in higher education should, as many do, expand their roles to consider life after college. Helping students prepare for the complex transition to life after graduation is an important responsibility shared by those in student affairs and others in higher education.

This chapter considers theories and models of practice that may inform how professionals contribute to students' transition to after-college life. The focus is on roles, self-authorship, socialization, transition, generations, and vocational development. By making use of these theories and models, the practitioner can more richly understand the impacts of time, space, and context on the experiences that students may have as they graduate from college and begin the next phase of their lives, whether continuing on to graduate or professional school, starting a first job, advancing a career, moving away from family, or simply completing their degree with no strict plan of what else may lie ahead. Student affairs professionals and faculty must understand how students see themselves and make meaning

NEW DIRECTIONS FOR STUDENT SERVICES, no. 138, Summer 2012 © Wiley Periodicals, Inc.
Published online in Wiley Online Library (wileyonlinelibrary.com) • DOI: 10.1002/ss.20003

of their own development in order to support them through the transition to life after college.

Role Acquisition Theory

Considering the various roles individuals play throughout their lives is important to understanding the way students shape relationships, goal-setting, decision-making, and identity throughout their college experience. Foundational cognitive and moral development theorists such as Arthur Chickering and Lawrence Kohlberg argue that the very way that traditional college-aged individuals learn to navigate the world and make decisions is based on fulfilling certain roles (Evans et al., 2010). How they may be perceived as a good son or daughter, the coolest friend, or the best student will motivate their behavior. They base decisions on what others expect or demand. As they develop a stronger sense of self, they learn to engage in behaviors that benefit the highest good, weighing the needs of others with their personal needs. Behavior becomes less directed by fulfilling roles and more by internal values. By the time these individuals reach college, they are in the midst of this developmental process. As they proceed to graduation, they will need to consider long-term personal and professional goals, and will have to mitigate their multiple roles with their own values and needs. To support them through their college experience, higher education professionals must consider the implications of transitioning from the role of student to that of graduate.

Role acquisition is a lifelong process. Robert K. Merton argues that each social role assumes a set of behaviors and expectations (1957). These expectations are set by society-at-large, media, and the legal system and are internalized by individuals and replicated by a reference group—others who share that same role. Merton pioneered the idea of role models, those who exemplify a certain role and its associated responsibilities and attributes. Each new social position connects an individual to an array of subsequent related roles (Yellin, 1999). Individuals do not simply conform to their various roles but rather interact with and shape them. Merton coined the term *self-fulfilling prophecy* to describe how an individual is able to shape an experience with ideas, whether external or internal, about one's abilities to perform a role. One may let external ideas infiltrate his/her thinking and determine their experience relevant to a certain role.

Merton's work is highly relevant to higher education. The college experience offers many opportunities for students to learn strategies to help them effectively navigate the dynamic process of role acquisition. Practitioners and professors may wish to think about opportunities to challenge students' behaviors or decision-making. Such challenges can help students think critically and more realistically about their ability to succeed in their various roles by crafting intentional experiences for reflection and

NEW DIRECTIONS FOR STUDENT SERVICES • DOI: 10.1002/ss

engagement, such as service learning or student-run events or clubs. Connecting a student's immediate interests to his or her long-term goals post-graduation may help the student reframe an understanding of a specific social role. Particular to preparing students for life after college, it is important to consider the various roles students are currently fulfilling and how those roles may change after graduation.

As student affairs professionals and their colleagues in higher education construct intentional experiences to support students as they prepare for after-college life, the importance of role modeling cannot be overlooked. As they progress on their path toward graduation and employment, students must see successful others to whom they can relate, whether on the basis of age, race, disability, sexual orientation, parent-status, or simply common interest. Knowing that others have successfully graduated may provide students with the personal motivation to also succeed. If a student is able to identify with another person who is succeeding in school or employment, he or she may believe such a goal is attainable. Creating opportunities for mentorship for college seniors or new graduate students may help spark that motivation.

To further conceptualize role acquisition, Thornton and Nardi (1975) identify four stages: anticipatory socialization, learning formal role expectations, learning informal role expectations, and developing personal role expectations. *Anticipatory socialization* is the period of time in which individuals aspiring to become members of a group begin to adopt group values to prepare for their transition into this group. Because the individual has not yet received formal training on this group membership, he must rely on informal education, (i.e., role modeling, media representation, familial expectations, etc.). As a result, the individual may develop a highly generalized understanding of group membership. If we apply Thornton and Nardi's model to the traditional college experience, we can appreciate the way a high school senior anticipates going off to college and what expectations they have about the mythical freshman year. The congruence between the anticipation and the reality of the experience will help determine the ease of the transition.

In the *learning formal role expectations* stage, one learns a new role from the inside. As it relates to college entry, role acquisition may include first-year orientation, professors' classroom expectations, residence hall standards, the fraternity pledge period, or the university's code of conduct. Role acquisition in this stage focuses on consensus and general opinion and does not yet allow for personal reaction to this new experience.

In the *learning informal role expectations stage*, the individual's personal opinions or responses become more relevant. Conflicts between the formal expectations and the informal expectations shape the specifics of an individual's experience. For example, the first-year student learns that they do not need to refer to their professor as doctor. The individual comes to recognize the liberties one is able to take, not only the strict expectations to which one is taught to adhere. Thornton and Nardi believe it is in this third stage that true transition and adjustment begin.

In the final stage, *developing personal role expectations*, the individual is able to express their own expectations. The individual will make sense of this new role and be able to develop personal strategies based on their own talents, strengths, and skills. For the first-year student, this could be the time when she develops effective study skills or joins a particular organization. The negotiation of the new role truly indicates acquisition.

As easily as Thornton and Nardi's model can be applied to transitioning into college, it can also be applied to the transition to after-college life. A student can benefit from considering the new role to which she or he will transition and appreciate that while preparation is important, it will not necessarily expedite the role acquisition or transition process. It may be helpful for the student to reflect on other transitions she or he has made and determine the positive and negative aspects of the experience.

The Theory of Self-Authorship

Marcia Baxter Magolda's theory of self-authorship is pertinent to understanding role acquisition. Baxter Magolda looked at developmental tasks associated with one's twenties, focusing on values exploration and determining one's path in life. She outlines four phases to self-authorship that move from external to internal self-definition: following formula, crossroads, becoming the author of one's life, and internal foundation (Evans et al., 2010). In the *following formula* phase, young adults define themselves by the plans laid out for them by external authorities. Gaining approval of others is central at this stage. This phase has implications for career choice and planning. Many young adults may simply do what they are supposed or expected to do, as opposed to being motivated by their personal preferences.

In the *crossroads* phase, individuals realize that the plans they have been following may not truly fit their needs. They may also be disappointed in the way others define them and start to resist the need for external approval. Here they may chart a new path that resonates more closely with their developing personal values. A new career setting is often the catalyst for this kind of questioning and internal conflict. The resolution of crossroads is a clearer sense of direction and increased self-confidence.

At the *becoming author of one's life* phase, individuals begin to live out their new goals and beliefs. As a result of the nascent sense of self-authorship, individuals are better able to mitigate conflicting external viewpoints.

In the final phase, *internal foundation*, individuals have a strong self-concept. They are able to handle ambiguity as well as change because they are grounded in their personal beliefs.

NEW DIRECTIONS FOR STUDENT SERVICES • DOI: 10.1002/ss

The theory of self-authorship explains experiences of those in their twenties and thirties and therefore is apt for understanding those students ready to transition out of college, or perhaps nontraditional students who decide to make changes to their educational or career paths. Self-authorship offers a new way to conceptualize the impact of social roles and provides context for those struggling with the impact of personal and professional choices.

The theories of role acquisition and self-authorship can be used in higher education in the areas of career and transition counseling. Working with students to identify expectations they have internalized from external sources may prove valuable in helping them clarify personal goals related to life after college. Helping students to appreciate the realities associated with graduation, a new job, or relocating is a way of fostering their preparation.

Socialization Theory

It is through both formal and informal processes, as well as personal reflection, that an individual learns a new role and how and where she or he fits within a new setting. In addition to focusing on the individual adjustment to a role, it can be helpful in understanding transitions to also focus on organizational culture and how we become socialized into various social and cultural arenas, including both education and the workplace.

Van Maanen and Schein (1979) pioneered research around organizational culture. They argue that beyond a specific position or job, there is a culture that comprises both formal and informal methods of doing things. Each organization has a history, a reputation, a chain of command, a language, and a process of recognition. They define organizational socialization as the way one learns the ropes (Van Maanen and Schein, 1979, p. 3). Van Maanen and Schein do not present this process as linear or simple. They argue that organizational socialization is complex and unique to each setting and individual.

Weidman, Twale, and Stein (2001) build upon Van Maanen and Schein's work to shed light upon the process of graduate and professional student socialization with the goal of informing graduate program faculty, administrators, and those professionals with oversight of our nation's graduate and professional programs. They define socialization as "the process by which persons acquire the knowledge, skills and dispositions necessary to make them more or less effective members of their society" (Weidman, Twale, and Stein, 2001, p. 4). Graduate and professional students are faced with the challenge of identifying with their roles as students in a new and specific academic culture, while simultaneously learning to identify with their future profession and professional culture.

Weidman, Twale, and Stein believe that socialization is both a common and individual experience for graduate students. For example, there is a common set of classes or skill sets required for all graduate students, but students conducting unique research have an individualized experience. Socialization is also formal and informal. Formal orientation or instruction is a mandatory component of graduate school, but so are the informal, casual ways that students learn from one another or create their own rites of passage.

Building upon the work of Thornton and Nardi, Weidman, Twale, and Stein put forth a four-stage model of graduate and professional student socialization: anticipatory, formal, informal, and personal. With each stage, a student becomes more entrenched in the academic culture and takes on increasing levels of responsibility with research, faculty involvement, and mentoring of other graduate students. Weidman, Twale, and Stein discuss core elements of socialization associated with each stage.

Knowledge acquisition is identified as a core element of socialization. Students must learn certain skills and information specific to their discipline and critical to their chosen professional role. They must also determine the level to which they are able to effectively meet the demands of their professional role. For example, a medical student may be extremely knowledgeable about specific subject matter, but she may be unable to work under pressure or for long hours with little sleep. During graduate or professional school, knowledge shifts from general to specific, and one begins the process of developing a professional identity. By the end of this education, the student will emerge as a member of a professional community. Understanding the responsibilities associated with this role is part of the socialization process.

The second core element is *investment*. As students become more entrenched in the academic and professional culture, they begin to dedicate more personal time to it. As one becomes increasingly committed to his field, it becomes difficult to consider changing educational or professional paths. At this point, the sponsorship of a faculty member is critically important to the success of the student (Weidman, Twale, and Stein, 2001). As Merton suggested, identifying a role model or mentor helps to increase personal accountability and overall commitment to the field.

The third core element is *involvement*. Theorists, most notably Astin (1984), have argued that the more involved a student is with his or her education or academic community, the more likely this student will be to succeed. Weidman, Twale, and Stein identify joining a professional organization, partnering with faculty research, or attending community forums as ways that students become involved in graduate and professional school. These types of involvement lead to increased awareness of both common and individual issues related to the profession and solidify one's identification with his professional role.

When considering Weidman, Twale, and Stein's contributions to graduate and professional student socialization, it is important to consider the role of the environment in this process. The authors discuss linear and nonlinear processes associated with socialization, thereby acknowledging that socialization is both a dynamic and interactive process.

Weidman, Twale, and Stein discuss the impact of diversity, access to technology, the experience of international students, and the cultural implications of ethics, professionalism, and professionalization as necessary to consider when thinking critically about socialization. These dynamics will shape the way an individual student experiences socialization. Each student will bring his or her own amount of cultural capital, approach each assignment or presentation with a personal cultural lens, and engage in each interaction with faculty and peers with this perspective. Students are not naive regarding cultural conflicts and dynamics of access and equity. Those helping to prepare students for after-college life should discuss these dynamics not only with them, but also with future graduate programs and potential employers.

Work can also be done to engage new graduate and professional students, be it student affairs or an academic discipline. Reaching out to new graduate students and creating opportunities for their meaningful participation on campus will contribute to their success during this transitional time (Gansemer-Topf, Ross, and Johnson, 2006).

Transition Theory

Perhaps it is appropriate to think about the college experience as a series of transitions. There is a great deal of focus in student affairs and higher education on understanding the initial transition to college and how a student becomes connected to campus. Many institutional structures are in place to ease this transition and provide community for new students, who are more likely to persist in college when they connect to campus (Astin, 1993; Tinto, 1994; Tierney, 2000). For example, residence halls, cultural centers, and fraternities and sororities provide smaller, more intimate communities for new university students to which they may become connected and through which they are held accountable. It is fair to say that this theory of involvement has been criticized for neglecting nontraditional students and students of diverse identities and backgrounds (Tierney, 2000).

There are a number of subsequent transitions along the path to graduation. Examples include moving from a residence hall to an apartment, taking on student employment, advancing from class to class, increasing leadership responsibilities within clubs or organizations, and choosing a major and delving into increasingly specific and difficult course work. With determination and support, these experiences culminate in a ceremony of transition—the pomp and circumstance of commencement. When we consider the root of the word *commencement*, it literally means to begin.

Nancy Schlossberg's (Schlossberg, Waters, and Goodman, 1977) model dedicated to understanding transition is widely respected and used in higher education as well as counseling, rehabilitation, and other fields. Schlossberg defines transition as any event or nonevent that results in changed relationships, routines, assumptions, and roles.

To make meaning of transition, Schlossberg suggests that one must understand the type, context, and impact of the transition. Transitions can be anticipated or nonanticipated and can also include nonevents. An anticipated event may be college graduation, while a nonanticipated event could be the sudden death of a parent. Both instances mark the start of a transition, but the expectations and preparation for each event are drastically different. A nonevent can also be an event that is anticipated but does not occur, like a student who applies for work and is not offered a position. Events such as graduating, applying for graduate school, relocating for a new job, and being offered work are truly what shape and define the complex process of transitioning to after-college life.

To help make meaning of transitional events, Schlossberg looks at the context of the transition. She defines context as one's relationship to the transition. For the purpose of this chapter, students are directly experiencing the transition out of college. College roommates, fraternity brothers, faculty, or parents may be involved in this transition but are not experiencing it directly. Further, Schlossberg looks at the level of impact the transition makes on the individual and others in that person's life. Impact is understood as the degree to which the transition affects daily life for the individual and those involved. Impact is determined by the individual and is therefore subjective.

The framework Schlossberg puts forth to understand an individual's ability to cope with transition revolves around situation, self, support, and strategies (commonly referred to as the 4S model). Assessing personal resources in each of these four areas may help to understand how and why individuals experience similar transitions differently. This is where the opportunities lie for practitioners and faculty. First, helping professionals can validate the transition to after-college life. Then, they can work with students on how to be proactive while preparing for graduation and life beyond. While nonanticipated events and nonevents may occur, transitions can be discussed and considered both before they happen and when they are taking place. Even simply mapping out various opportunities, options, and implications may provide a road map to empower students to navigate this potentially tumultuous time.

Regarding nonanticipated or nonevents, it may be helpful to talk with students about stress management and coping skills. While one hopes for only the best outcomes relevant to graduation, job searching, and admission to graduate schools, it is important to talk with students about how to handle disappointing or stressful events such as a rejection from a graduation program or even a drawn-out, confusing professional selection process.

NEW DIRECTIONS FOR STUDENT SERVICES • DOI: 10.1002/ss

On-Time and Off-Time Events

The work of Beatrice Neugarten can also be useful in informing practice related to helping students with transition. Neugarten looks at the meaning of age and how age is a major organizational dimension of society (Neugarten and Neugarten, 1996). Neugarten posits that age is a significant factor in how people form judgments about others, interpret behavior, and measure themselves. For example, throughout their lives, and particularly their schooling, children are judged by how well they are doing for their age. Norms around age exist, and they serve to socialize people with respect to age-appropriate behavior. Age divides our lifetimes into phases that are marked by personal and professional milestones such as college graduation.

According to Neugarten, "our changing society has brought with it changes in the social meaning of age: blurred boundaries between the periods of life, new definitions of age groups, new patterns in the timing of major life events and new inconsistencies in what is considered age-appropriate behavior" (Neugarten, 1996, p. 72). Individuals whose behaviors and actions are congruent with societal norms and expectations are considered to be *on-time* while those who are in not in line with them are *off-time*.

Student affairs professionals, faculty members, and other colleagues should consider that graduation may not hold the same meaning for all students. While the majority of college students will follow a similar path to graduation, Neugarten's work has particular implications for adult college students, student parents, and those whose path to college from high school has been disrupted, like student veterans or those who may have experienced a traumatic event. For nontraditional students, graduation may hold a very different meaning and elicit different personal or emotional responses. Nevitt Sanford encourages higher education professionals to meet students where they are developmentally. Based on the complexity of transition and the various experiences student encounter leading up to graduation, professionals must be sensitive (as cited in Evans et al., 2010) and challenge themselves to work with students to authentically understand their goals for graduating and not assume the personal value or significance of the event.

Generations

It is important to consider the unique characteristics of each graduating class to effectively support them as they prepare for the transition to life after college. William Howe and Neil Strauss (2000) have contributed much to the conversation on collegiate cohorts through their work on generations. Perhaps most relevant is their work on Millennials. How today's undergraduates approach their college experiences or their after-college roles as graduate or transfer students, new professionals, and community members is shaped by the generation into which they were born.

A generation is generally defined by a specific time period and common experiences (Elam, Stratton, and Gibson, 2007). Members of a generation share an understanding of significant people, places, and events—indicators that shape values, personal traits, goals, and roles. According to Howe and Strauss (2000), members of five generations account for the vast majority of the United States' population: the G.I. generation (1902–1924), the Silent generation (1925–1942), the Boomer generation (1943–1960), Generation X (1961–1981), and the Millennial generation (1982–2002). The majority of students currently enrolled at institutions of higher education are members of either Generation X or the Millennial generation (Howe and Strauss, 2000).

It is important to understand the characteristics of the Millennials to see how they perceive their college experience and the transition to life after college. An authentic understanding of their goals and values will also shed light on what they need and expect from higher education professionals during this time. The Millennials' world view has been shaped by events such as: Operation Desert Storm; the Columbine High School shootings; the advent of reducing, reusing, and recycling; technology in the classroom; instant communication; and highly involved parents, teachers, and coaches who are generous with praise and recognition. Carney Strange (2004) summarizes seven defining characteristics ascribed to Millennials by Howe and Strauss (2000):

1. Structured rule followers
2. Protected and sheltered
3. Confident and optimistic
4. Conventionally motivated and respectful
5. Cooperative and team-oriented
6. Pressured by and accepting of authority
7. Talented achievers

In addition to their many positive attributes, Millennials can demonstrate challenging behaviors to higher education professionals. They can be demanding of time and expect instant feedback. Also their increased reliance on their parents and technology may negatively affect their communication and interpersonal skills as well as their sense of personal responsibility (Elam, Stratton, and Gibson, 2007).

Understanding how millennial students who are preparing for after-college life perceive this transition can inform the way higher education professionals can be effective supports during this time. Because they are team-oriented and cooperative, a class or workshop experience might be useful in gathering together to process the transition out of college. With a professional instructor or advisor, students could discuss plans and goals, and also learn in a supportive environment how to prepare for graduate exams, interviews, and challenges as first-time professionals. Because of their comfort with technology, it might be helpful to incorporate an online component to this class, and incorporate lessons on how to use the Internet responsibly as they transition into the role of new graduate student or new professional. Since Millennials have grown up with regular recognition and special attention, they may appreciate a celebration to commemorate the end of their college experience.

While the majority of American undergraduates are Millennials, it would be a disservice to ignore how events like graduation and the transition out of college may affect other nontraditional, non-Millennial students. These students may not want expansive graduation celebrations, but may experience this process on a more individual basis. They may not be as driven by rules and protocol as their Millennial counterparts; hence, professionals will need to develop specific strategies to motivate them through graduation and all the consequent tasks and responsibilities, such as choosing a graduate school or a career path.

Vocational Theory

When considering the transition from college to career, research provides relevant insight. Not only are there major changes in roles, cultures, and routine, the challenges of transition are exacerbated by the lack of skills and experiences necessary to be successful at work (Wendlandt and Rochlen, 2008). Over one's lifetime, one may hold many positions and professions. Each career change requires coping skills and a level of resiliency or adaptability (Murphy et al., 2010). Theories have been developed to understand career development; they not only analyze individual characteristics and occupational tasks relevant to career choice and success but also the personal development that occurs over time.

Donald Super (1980) contributed much to career development research with his work on the development of self-concept. His life-span, life-space theory of careers argues that self-concept changes over time and as a result of various life experiences (Super, 1980). Hence, career development is a lifelong, dynamic, and unique process. Super proposed five stages to explain life and career development starting at birth and spanning a lifetime: growth, exploration, establishment, maintenance, and decline. During the *growth* stage, one is developing a self-concept, values, and a general understanding of the professional world. One then *explores* various vocations through classes and hobbies. According to Super, around the ages of 25–44 is when one typically becomes *established* in a career. After this, in the *maintenance* stage, one works to improve in his or her field. In Super's last stage, *decline*, the individual prepares for retirement and begins contributing less to his/her field. People will cycle through these stages as they switch positions and undergo career transitions.

Mark Savickas (1997) introduced the idea of adaptability as key to successfully navigating career development and offered it as a substitute for vocational maturity. According to Savickas, adaptability, rather than maturity, more aptly captures the interaction between person and environment. Using the construct of adaptability, an individual is able to respond productively to his or her environment and will be increasingly able to implement their self-concepts in their work situations (1997). Given the dynamic nature of today's professional world with increased globalization, integration of technology, multicultural communication, and compromised personal-professional boundaries, one's ability to adapt is critical to professional success.

Higher education professionals most likely work with students moving from exploration to establishment. College students of any age are likely exploring their interests by taking electives, engaging in leadership opportunities, completing internships, or other curricular or cocurricular experiences. They are selecting a career path and hoping that it will be appropriate in the long term. Murphy and colleagues (2010, p. 174) quote Eric Erikson, whose contributions to social psychology lay the foundation for developmental theory, as observing it is "primarily the inability to settle on an occupational identity which disturbs young people." Student affairs professionals may be able to offer support to those grappling with these questions.

John Holland's Theory of Vocational Personalities and Environments (1959) explains career choice and job satisfaction. He asserts that people choose certain vocations based on their personalities and are attracted to work environments that reflect this personality. Holland's typology indicator identifies personal strengths, interests, and affinities relevant to work. He identifies six personality types and work environments: realistic, investigative, artistic, social, enterprising, and conventional. He argues that the closer the match of personality to job, the greater the job satisfaction. While typology indicators are criticized for being overly simplistic, they do offer opportunities to reflect and connect personality with potential careers. All individuals are complex and possess pieces of each personality type identified by Holland. It is important for one to think about personal affinity to certain situations and how to connect personality type to different occupations.

Higher education professionals can work with students to discover their preferences, assets, and liabilities relevant to choosing a career path. Because typology indicators are fairly simple to understand, students may be able to reflect on their results and use them to inform how to select a major, an internship, a first job, or a graduate or professional program. Holland's theory may be incorporated into a senior seminar class that helps prepare students for graduation or serve as the basis for a student program, perhaps with involvement from Career Services or student leadership staff.

Conclusion

This chapter presents theories and models of practice relevant to the transitions students experience in their lives that may be applied to the very sensitive and important transition to after-college life that is often neglected in professional practice in higher education. These works all suggest that transition is a process. Students should prepare themselves for upcoming transitions; however, much of the true adjustment will occur once they are experiencing and negotiating their new roles.

Responsible professionals must perpetually ask which student demographics are represented in theory and which are not. The experience of transitioning out of college may be different for students of diverse cultural identities, those who are not of traditional age, or those who have experienced life-altering events. For many students, their affiliation to various cultural groups or fiscal or family responsibilities will often shape their academic and career choices. This underscores the importance of role models with whom students can authentically identify, who can inspire their success, and good mentors who can motivate them through the unique challenges associated with role acquisition and transition.

Student affairs staff, faculty, and others in higher education can easily enhance the experiences of new graduate students and professionals by providing opportunities for their orientation and involvement on campus. It may also be prudent to consider the boundaries of our institutions, and how they are situated in their communities. Colleges and universities have an opportunity to educate prospective employers on the student experience and their transition out of college. This work can be done through campus-facilitated business advisory councils, workshops, online resources, or through building relationships with companies participating in career fairs. By addressing the experiences of diverse and nontraditional students as part of these educational efforts, employers may better understand their new employees as well as the level of inclusiveness in their own professional culture. This leadership on the part of institutions of higher education has the potential to enhance recruitment of new employees and also to lay successful inroads for the transition to the working world.

Theory can provide higher education professionals a foundation upon which to build. Keeping in mind the major insights and tools theory can provide, professionals in higher education can craft programmatic and curricular interventions to serve as intentional opportunities to engage students and empower them to manage their transitions out of college and prepare them for what is to come after graduation. The next few chapters discuss programmatic and curricular interventions that seek to prepare students for after-college life. Various approaches will be introduced and their applications analyzed through the use of case studies.

References

Astin, A. *What Matters in College: Four Critical Years Revisited.* San Francisco: Jossey-Bass, 1993.

Astin, A. W. "Student Involvement: A Developmental Theory for Higher Education." *Journal of College Student Personnel, 25,* 1984.

Elam, C., Stratton, T., and Gibson, D. "Welcoming a New Generation to College: The Millennial Students." *Journal of College Admission,* Spring 2007.

Evans, N. J., Forney, D. S., Guido, F. M., Patton, L. D., and Renn, K. A. *Student Development in College: Theory, Research, and Practice* (2nd ed.). San Francisco: Jossey-Bass, 2010.

Gansemer-Topf, A. M., Ross, L. E.,and Johnson, R. M. (2006). "Graduate and Professional Student Development and Student Affairs." In M. J. Guentzel and B. E. Nesheim (eds.), *Supporting Graduate and Professional Students: The Role of Student Affairs* (New Directions for Student Services #115). San Francisco: Jossey-Bass, 2006.

Holland, J. L. "A Theory of Vocational Choice." *Journal of Career Psychology, 6*(1), 1959.

Howe, N., and Strauss, W. *Millennials Rising: The Next Great Generation.* New York: Vintage Books, 2000.

Merton, R. K. *Social Theory and Social Structure.* New York: The Free Press, 1957.

Murphy, K. A., Blustein, D. L., and Bohlig, A. "The College-to-Career Transition: An Exploration of Emerging Adulthood." *The Journal of Counseling and Development, 88,* 2010.

Neugarten, B. L., and Neugarten, D. A. *The Meanings of Age: Selected Papers of Bernice L. Neugarten.* Chicago: The University of Chicago Press, 1996.

Pascarella, E. T., and Terenzini, P. T. *How College Affects Students* (2nd ed.). San Francisco: Jossey-Bass, 2005.

Savickas, M. L. "Career Adaptability: An Integrative Construct for Life-Span Theory." *Career Development Quarterly, 45,* 1997.

Schlossberg, N. K., Waters, E. B., and Goodman, J. *Counseling Adults in Transition* (2nd ed.). New York: Springer, 1977.

Strange, C. C. "Constructions of Student Development across the Generations." In M. D. Coomes and R. DeBard (eds.), *Serving the Millennial Generation* (New Directions in Student Services, #106). San Francisco: Jossey-Bass, 2004.

Super, D. (1980). "A Life-Span, Life-space Approach to Career Development." *Journal of Vocational Behavior, 16*(30), 282–298.

Thornton, R., and Nardi, P. (1975). The Dynamics of Role Acquisition. *The American Journal of Sociology, 80*(4), 870–885.

Tierney, W. G. "Power, Identity and the Dilemma of College Student Departure." In J. M. Braxton (ed.), Reworking the Student Departure Puzzle (pp. 213–234). Nashville, TN: Vanderbilt University Press, 2000.

Tinto, V. *Leaving College: Rethinking the Causes and the Cures of Student Attrition.* Chicago: University of Chicago Press, 1994.

Van Maanen, J., and, Schein, E. H. "Toward a Theory of Organizational Socialization." *Research in Organizational Behavior, 1,* 1979.

Weidman, J. C., Twale, D. J., and Stein, E. L. "Socialization of Graduate and Professional Students in Higher Education: A Perilous Passage?" *ASHE-ERIC Higher Education Report*, 28(3). New York: John Wiley & Sons, 2001.

Wendlandt, N. M., and Rochlen, A. B. "Addressing the College-to-Work Transition: Implications for University Career Counselors." *Journal of Career Development* 35(2), 2008.

Yellin, L. L. "Role Acquisition as a Social Process." *Sociological Inquiry* 69(2), 1999.

AMANDA KRAUS is an adjunct faculty member of Higher Education at the University of Arizona. She serves as assistant director at the University's Disability Resource Center.

3

Programs are one avenue for preparing students for after-college life. General principles, theories, and examples of such programs are discussed here.

Pathway Programs to Life after College

Jim F. McAtee

Louisa May Alcott boldly stated, "I'm not afraid of storms, for I'm preparing to sail my ship" (Ryan, 1996, p. 69). Like Alcott, college students are preparing for their journey beyond college. The transition from college to whatever lies ahead can be exciting and scary for them. How the transition experience unfolds for students will be the result of a combination of factors including individual circumstances, how the student responds to change and unknown expectations, and how well they are prepared and informed for their transition. While it can be difficult to affect individual circumstances, well-crafted programming can be helpful in shaping how well students respond and how well they are prepared and informed. This chapter explores programming used to prepare students for the transition to various next steps in their lives, including from community college to university, from undergraduate years to graduate school, from university to work, and from university to military. Program examples are given and topics for future consideration are presented.

Theories and Models

Chapter Two provides an overview of theories related to helping prepare students for life after college, but it may be helpful in this chapter to address two theories in particular. First, in talking about transition programs, it seems relevant to revisit Schlossberg's Transition Theory (Schlossberg, 1984). It provides us with a model that can be used to assist students through transitions. That model is based on four constructs that are commonly referred to as the 4 Ss: situation, self, supports, and strategies. How a student reacts to a transition is affected by each of the four. Whether or not a student has undergone similar experiences, whether or not the event is perceived to be on time or off time (Neugarten, 1979), and

New Directions for Student Services, no. 138, Summer 2012 © Wiley Periodicals, Inc.
Published online in Wiley Online Library (wileyonlinelibrary.com) • DOI: 10.1002/ss.20004

29

whether or not the student perceives the situation as voluntary or coerced all affect the meaning they make of the *situation*. The inner strength and experiences of an individual are critical elements in coping with transitions; this is *self*. The *supports* a student has, such as the availability of people, services, resources, and agencies, are critical elements in the ability to cope with transitions. *Strategies*, the fourth and final construct, refers to the identification of various options for action.

Harris-Bowlsbey, Suddarth, and Reile (2008) offer a useful guide for career services professionals interested in making use of Schlossberg's work to help students. They suggest specific questions that may be posed to students as a way of helping them divide up what appears to be a complex or overwhelming transition into the four discrete and manageable constructs. Programming that helps students develop an inventory for themselves of each of the four constructs as it relates to their upcoming transition can be both helpful and reassuring.

The second theory revisited here is the work of Chickering and Reisser (1993). In one of the seminal works in student affairs, Chickering and Reisser identify seven developmental vectors. The sixth vector, *developing purpose*, has particular importance as it relates to preparing students for life after college. Purpose for students can revolve around career goals, personal aspirations, commitment to family, or other aspects of life, including religion or service to country. Programming that can help students explore and develop their purpose can lead them to a transition that is more clear and seems more attainable.

Defining Programming

Barr and Keating (1985) define programming as "a theoretically based plan, under which action is taken toward a goal within the context of institutions of higher education" (p. 3). While Barr and Keating offer a definition, Barr and Cuyjet (as cited in Cuyjet, 1996) offer a three-part typology of program types that fits different programming models shared in this chapter:

1. Delivery of specific activities or services by a unit
2. Series of planned interventions developed for a defined target population or to meet a specific goal
3. One-time activities with a planned target and purpose (pp. 398–399)

Types of Transitions and Programming to Support Students

Each transition has its own set of challenges, emotions, and rewards that is associated with moving a student's life plan forward. Some of the challenges and emotions are similar across all transitions, while others are unique. One commonality is that there is a level of excitement and anxiety that accompanies any transition. The better one is prepared, the easier it is to have a successful transition.

In each of the transitions addressed in this chapter, students are expected to apply past experiences to successfully navigate future challenges. For example, a student transferring from a community college to a university, or vice versa, is expected to have learned from previous college experiences how to study and retain information. A student transitioning from an undergraduate program to a graduate program is expected to know how to research and use multiple pieces of existing knowledge to create questions leading to the discovery of new knowledge. A student leaving academic pursuits in search of a career and job is expected to know how to be a lifelong learner, what employers want in a new employee, and how to be successful in their chosen profession. A student who was in the Reserve Officer Training Corps (ROTC) program is expected to have an understanding of the military culture and to apply that knowledge to meet military expectations. The following sections present information regarding preparing students for these expectations of transitioning to the next stage in their lives.

Community College to University

In 2007–2008 there were 609,016 degrees awarded by the 1,167 American community colleges (American Association of Community Colleges, 2011). It is difficult to say what an average transfer rate would be because the reporting guidelines for community colleges vary across the nation. However, a rough range is between 30 percent and 60 percent (Palmer, 2011).

The U.S. Department of Education's Office of Vocational and Adult Education states that there appear to be two key factors that facilitate the transfer process (Office of Vocational and Adult Education, 2008). One of these two factors is articulation agreements, and Chapter Five addresses this topic. The other factor is the types of academic and social support programs and services offered. This section will focus on the academic and social programs.

To assist students in successfully transferring, many community colleges and universities offer support programs and resources. For example, some community colleges and universities participate in transfer fairs. Transfer fairs involve universities with articulation agreements visiting the community colleges with whom they partner. These fairs are intended to introduce students to the programs universities have to which students can transfer. Transfer fairs also meet the needs of the institutions to market programs and services directly to potential students. These programs deliver specific activities for a target population to meet the goal of facilitating transfers. Partners in transfer fairs can include numerous departments and service providers such as admissions, advising, financial aid, career services, academic departments, student housing, and student life.

NEW DIRECTIONS FOR STUDENT SERVICES • DOI: 10.1002/ss

The success of transfer programs is measured largely by the percent of those who transfer from a community college to a university and then graduate (Office of Vocational and Adult Education, 2008). Graduation rates and retention rates are receiving more attention as institutions of higher education address budget challenges. Some states like North Carolina (Wiser, 2010) have begun to tie funding at universities to retention and graduation rates. If the goal is not reached, funding may be limited or even reduced (Associated Press, 2010). This creates a challenge for universities because the graduation rate for students who transfer from community college seems to be low.

There are ways to make the transition from community college to university more successful and therefore have a positive affect on retention and graduation rates. One example is the Puente Project (2011) in California, which serves as a comprehensive intervention program that operates at the community college level. The goal is to increase those who transfer to four-year colleges and universities from educationally underserved student populations. The Puente Project helps facilitate the transfer of underprivileged students through mentoring, rigorous instruction, and focused academic counseling. The program trains high school and community college instructors and counselors on how to provide programming focused on mentoring, rigorous instruction, and academic counseling. The program's components are developed specifically for the purpose of assisting and preparing students to transfer to the next level of their education.

Having well-marketed and accessible transfer centers at the community college level aids in the success of student transitions from community college to university. As stated earlier, most of this responsibility is placed on the shoulders of the academic counselors. Some universities and community colleges will partner to provide a transfer counselor who will reside part time on the university campus and part time on the community college campus. The Crossroads Program, a partnership between Indiana University–Purdue University Fort Wayne and Ivy Tech Northeast, utilizes this approach.

Another way for community colleges and universities to partner is a transfer counselor day. For example, the University of Akron holds such a program, and counselors at community colleges from which students transfer are hosted at the university. The counselors are given a tour of the university, learn about the academic programs, and make connections they can utilize when they have questions.

While some universities bring community college counselors to their campuses and some share counselors between their institutions to help facilitate the transfer process, others like Colorado State University have entire student centers dedicated to assisting transfer students. Colorado State University helps transfer students through the Transfer Student Center. After attending a Transfer Orientation Session, the students can make appointments with a transfer student counselor through their

TransCentral program. Colorado State University also hosts a Transfer Student Visit Day. From 9 A.M. to 4 P.M., attendees participate in panel discussions including transfer policies and current transfer students' experiences. Lunch is provided, and attendees are exposed to the different departments on campus that can help them and answer their questions.

A common approach to providing support for transfer students is to have an online tool that helps students and their family members to navigate the transfer process. As first-generation students, and even those who are not first-generation students, and family members learn about the processes and resources to facilitate a successful transfer, they may encounter many unfamiliar academic terms. Transfer resources can play a vital role in explaining and demystifying those terms and in clearly describing the transfer pathway. One example of such a resource is www .transferin.net, which provides a particularly helpful "Terms to Know" resource.

Students can transfer to another institution as a junior, but also as a sophomore, freshman, senior, or graduate student. The transition from undergraduate to graduate student is different from transferring from one undergraduate program to another. Even though the graduate student may be advancing their education at the same institution, there are transitions that take place when moving from undergraduate studies to graduate studies.

Undergraduate to Graduate Studies

The transition from undergraduate studies to graduate studies is largely one of moving from the consumption of knowledge to the production of knowledge. This can be a large leap for students who have been in undergraduate programs that have not prepared them for this shift in purpose. For many years such students have looked to the professor to feed them knowledge to remember and apply. Some students feel inadequate to step into the role of knowledge producer after being a knowledge consumer for many years.

Creating a community of undergraduate studies can help to create the support that graduate students need in this transition. Faculty relationships and graduate assistantships play a key role as well. There are programs that are administered in each graduate program, such as orientation. Graduate School Orientation is where student expectations ought to be set by the graduate school, and students can ask questions and learn about resources to help them be successful in their programs.

On a federal level TRIO programs are designed to identify and provide services for individuals from disadvantaged backgrounds (Office of Postsecondary Education, 2011). There are eight programs under the TRIO umbrella, including the Ronald E. McNair Postbaccalaureate Achievement Program. The Ronald E. McNair program is named after astronaut Ronald

McNair, who died in the 1986 Challenger space shuttle explosion. There are over 230 McNair programs across the United States (U.S. Department of Education, 2011).

The program targets students from disadvantaged backgrounds including first-generation college students, minority groups, and those who have socioeconomic challenges as related to obtaining advanced degrees. Participants must be recognized as having a disadvantaged background and must have shown strong academic potential (Office of Vocational and Adult Education, 2011). The goal of this program is to increase representation of those who have attained a PhD degree and are from an underrepresented segment of society. As students complete their undergraduate work, institutions work closely with the students and encourage them to enroll in graduate programs.

McNair projects have certain required activities, including opportunities for research, internships, educational opportunities that enhance preparation for doctoral study, tutoring, academic counseling, and assistance in enrolling in graduate school, including admission and financial assistance. Other recommended components include financial and economic literacy, mentoring programs, and exposure to cultural events not usually available to students who are classified as disadvantaged.

Other common programs include mentor programs, workshops, colloquia, and summer camps for undergraduates who were preparing for graduate studies. Assistance with application preparation, including letters of interest, is often offered through writing centers and career services offices. Among other services, most career services offices assist with cover letter writing and letters of interest or statements of purpose often required by graduate school applications.

University to Work

Study after study shows that the number-one reason students go to a university is to get a job. When you take that high salience and couple it with the high stress resulting from the current economic situation, you can see why this is an important area on which to focus. With references to the new economic environment worldwide, students who see their parents lose their jobs and who are aware of rising prices and economic crises can find the university-to-work transition to be one of the most terrifying steps they will make. Unlike other transitions, this is one transition in which students do not have a specified course catalog to follow, a crosswalk to show them how their past efforts translate to future classes, or a senior officer to play reveille to awake them in the morning.

There are many programs available to assist students in the transition from university to work. These programs range from formal programs such as Workkeys and NCRC (Nationally Recognized Career Readiness Certificate) programs to general workshops led by career services offices and other offices in partnership with career services. Some programs are very structured, and some are less structured and offered only when requested. Others are integrated into classrooms and part of the syllabus and grading process for classes.

Some common program topics include mock interviews, service learning, internships, and job shadows. Workshops that train students regarding resumes, cover letters, thank-you notes, job-search strategies, networking, and salary negotiation are also common. Career and job fairs are common, as are programs to prepare students for successful career fair participation. For instance, few students know that many employers do not accept hard-copy resumes and insist instead that students apply online. A resume is still required, but if students are not made aware of the expectations ahead of time, they can become discouraged.

Less common programs include mentoring programs in partnership with alumni associations and other professional partner groups, salary negotiation training, and programs for alumni that help with career changers and unemployed alumni. While these programs are less common, they are just as important as the more widely established programs.

East Carolina University, with an enrollment of over 24,000, offers a mock interview program that serves 1,300 students per year. This program is integrated into some of the core courses open to all majors and all class levels. Presentations are given in the classrooms. During the class presentations, training about the expectations of the program and the actual interview process is provided. The students are then given a deadline to sign up for the program. It is the student's responsibility to sign up, research a career choice, and then prepare for and complete the interview. Grading is based on the student's attendance and completion, not necessarily on how well the student interviewed.

Volunteers are used to conduct the 650 hours of mock interviewing. All reporting to the instructors is handled through the career center. This is an example of academic departments and career services collaborating to provide programming that prepares students for the transition from university to work. The interviewers give feedback to the interviewees and sometimes become mentors for the students through the process. Thus, although mock interview programs seek to teach this skill, often students are able to practice the skill of networking as well.

Indiana University–Purdue University Fort Wayne offers a job shadow program over spring break and places students in two- to three-day experiences with local companies. The students have a short assignment while on-site, and site visits are made by the career services office to follow up on the placement and the progress of the student. Job shadow programs help with the transition from university to work by exposing students to an experience to prepare them for entering the workforce. Even if students do not participate in any other experiential learning activity, a job shadow will give them a brief glimpse into what a work environment looks like outside of their classroom, and they will have the opportunity to observe behaviors in the workplace.

Career fairs are offered as a form of transition program, but few people outside of career services view them as developmental tools. Most see career fairs as focused on placement and recruitment. In contrast to this, career services encourages students to go to career fairs even if they are not looking for work. Career fairs are a safe place for students to practice approaching employers and carrying on a professional conversation. Students can take advantage of this relationship-building and networking tool before they need a job. As with interviewing skills, networking is a learned skill. The skills used to search for a job, conduct an interview, and network are improved with practice. The more rehearsing a student can have before they are put in a situation where their performance can make or break an opportunity for a job, the better.

Earlier there was mention of less common programs offered in partnership between career services and alumni associations. One of the programs offered in partnership between these two offices is commonly called Real Life 101. The contents of this program are offered in various ways, but usually with the same topics. Most Real Life 101 programs offer information about job searches, 401(k) plans, financial management, planning to pay back college loans, how to buy a home, choosing insurance, the power of compound interest, taxes, and other topics.

The experts in the various Real Life 101 topics are part of a panel or breakout sessions and they present and answer questions for seniors and recent alumni. Usually the presenters targeted are alumni of the school sponsoring the program. These programs are usually held in the spring about a month before graduation ceremonies. The office of career services usually plays a large role in these programs, and, along with the other topics presented, career services offers resume reviews, job hunt tips, and an economic and labor market overview.

As reported by the United States Department of Labor, in July 2010 the unemployment rate for those 16 to 24 years of age was 48.9 percent, equating to 18.6 million youth who are unemployed (Bureau of Labor Statistics, 2010). Another statistic to be aware of is the internship conversion rate. This measures the percent of interns that are hired full time at their internship employer. In 2005 the conversion rate was 35 percent. In 2009 the conversion rate rose to 58.6 percent (Koc, 2010). Looking at the 16- to 24-year-old unemployment rate and then taking notice of the trend for employers to hire students full time through their internship pipeline provides support for the argument that experiential learning opportunities are important. More than half of the students who were in an internship in 2009 did not have to conduct a job search.

Experiential learning programs come in an assortment of program models. Internship, cooperative education, service learning, externship, and job shadow programs are all examples of experiential learning. Some work-study and graduate assistantships follow the principles of experiential learning, but are not held to the same education component as the others. Some of these terms are used interchangeably by employers, students, faculty, and student affairs professionals. The reality is that they are different programs with different sets of goals and target populations.

Internship programs are flexible in that the length of the assignment and the structure of the academic component vary, and internships can be for credit or not for credit. Internships are also for pay or not for pay, as long as the employer follows the six guiding principles for nonpaid labor as defined by the United States Department of Labor Fact Sheet #71 (U.S. Department of Labor, 2010).

Cooperative education programs have a focused academic component and are usually offered for credit. Some programs offer cooperative education as a not-for-credit option, but in reality these would be more accurately defined as internships. Students can earn credit for documented learning outcomes that take place in the employment of a business. Cooperative education programs can be alternating or parallel. Alternating programs allow students to work one semester full time, and then attend school full time the next. Parallel programs allow students to work 15 to 20 hours per week while taking classes.

Externships and job shadow programs place students, and sometimes faculty and teachers from high schools, with employers who will host them for a half day to a full week, depending on the program. The student or educator will get an introduction to the employer and career about which they are interested in learning more.

Service learning combines education with community service. Service learning programs strive to balance student-learning outcomes for the classroom with providing a community service. Along with the student learning outcomes, students are exposed to the benefits of getting involved in the local community and what it means to be a good member of the local community. Students learn about the connection between their service and their academic coursework, as well as their role as citizens.

All of the experiential learning programs mentioned assist students with their transitions and in developing their purpose. Some are more structured than others, while some have a stronger academic component. All of the programs seek to prepare students to successfully navigate their transitions from university to the world of work.

University to Military

Those students who seek to prepare for the transition from university to military and pursue the military as a career path or at least for the amount of time they enlist can participate in the Reserve Officers Training Corps (ROTC) program. ROTC is intended to produce officers in all branches of the United States Military except the Coast Guard. The ROTC program prepares students to leave the university and enter the military as an officer. If in their sophomore year students choose not to contract with the military, they will still have gained valuable skills that will serve them in the civilian world.

Being in ROTC can be compared to taking an elective. It does not interfere with other classes a student may be taking to earn a specific degree. The traditional study time a student would normally spend studying for a class is spent in leadership and training events. These hands-on exercises help train and prepare ROTC participants for the challenges ahead.

Because the ROTC participants are paid during their time in the program, the need to focus on part-time jobs is not as important. This allows students in ROTC to focus more on their studies and trainings (personal interview with Sergeant First Class Corey Jenkins, ROTC Liaison Indiana Army National Guard). The trainings the participants take part in and lead are hands-on scenarios that they will face in the future. This is similar to the experiential learning goals of internships and co-ops, but at a higher intensity.

To prepare students for the transition from university to military, students in the freshmen and sophomore years take basic leadership classes and other classes that familiarize students with the military language and culture. The training is less hands-on in the freshman and sophomore years than in the junior and senior years.

Before the junior year starts, cadets (students in the ROTC program) must dedicate themselves to the military and sign a contract. If they choose not to contract with the military, they continue their civilian studies. Once students sign their contract, they are placed into leadership roles where they must practice in the field what they have learned.

More advanced cadets are expected to train, delegate authority to, and mentor less advanced cadets. They write very detailed step-by-step operational orders, and then they carry out the orders they have written. Cadets are sent on limited operations and rotate leadership roles. Each cadet has a turn at leading the squad on the brief operations.

Everything to this point in a student's ROTC training has been in preparation for the Leader Development and Assessment Course (LDAC). The LDAC is a five-week summer course to evaluate and train all ROTC Cadets (ROTC Leader Development and Assessment Course). Cadets go to Fort Lewis, Washington, to participate in the course between their junior and senior year.

The Army ROTC program has an evaluation system for their cadets. Cadets are evaluated by their cadre. Cadre members are officers and personnel who motivate and advise the ROTC battalion. Because the battalion is run by the cadets, the cadre serve as advisors and motivators for the battalion, helping the battalion cadets and leaders prepare for future commissioning in the military.

NEW DIRECTIONS FOR STUDENT SERVICES • DOI: 10.1002/ss

The evaluation process and outcomes are implemented through a series of cadre assessments and cadet reflections. When a cadet executes a skill, his or her performance is rated by the cadre. The cadet also conducts a self-evaluation of the performance. The evaluation also includes comparison of the ratings completed by both the cadre and the student. If there is need for explanation as to what would constitute a specific rating for a specific level of skill demonstration, the cadre can consult pre-established performance metrics and rubrics.

Looking Forward

As budgets become more of a factor in program continuation, so do the outcomes of transition programs. Some programs can show outcomes within a reasonable timeframe. Other programs do not see the fruits of their efforts until after the student transitions and is well into the activities of the next step in their journey. Showing results for transition programs can be challenging because institutions sometimes lose track of students and their progress after they transition beyond direct interaction and communication. Also, as found when researching the success rates of students who transition from community college to university, uniformity of reporting procedures between institutions can hinder the measurement of outcomes.

Looking forward, transition programs will need to evolve their delivery processes and assessment procedures to be sure they are addressing the changing needs of the student population. Also, data collection and analysis related to outcomes will need to have robust and effective methods in place, to ensure that the goals of the program are being met for the good of the students, and second, to be able to show the value of the program so that it can become sustainable and funded. This requires partnerships beyond the entity that administers the program, to include the place to which the student will be transitioning.

Many institutions use evaluations that indicate the level of satisfaction with programming. More emphasis needs to be placed on learning outcomes and how these are applied after the transition has been completed. Only then will we really know how effective the programs were in preparing students for the challenges they will face in any given transition. This type of assessment requires long-term partnerships and commitment from multiple partners at different times throughout a student's academic and postacademic career. Because of natural attrition at the different institutions that would make these types of partnerships possible, the process of follow-up and assessment between partners needs to be institutionalized and systemic. One example of this would be articulation agreements between academic institutions. Similar partnerships among businesses, military, and other partners where student transitions take place could be helpful in capturing the data needed to properly assess and analyze data.

As programs are being asked to validate their existence, more outcome assessments and a cycle of improvement for programs will become essential to continue important transition programs for students. If a program could report that the success of students who navigated a particular transition was directly related to the functions and actions of the transition program, then it would be beneficial to students and partners to continue the program.

Effectively exploring programming that can affect successful transitions embraces a focus on an assessment program that includes student learning outcomes and a cycle of improvement that utilizes the analysis of the data to continuously update programming. One way to explore these outcomes is through case studies. The next chapter provides case studies that showcase transition programming.

References

American Association of Community Colleges. "Fast Facts." Retrieved June 20, 2011, from http://www.aacc.nche.edu/AboutCC/Pages/fastfacts.aspx, 2011.

Associated Press. "Tracking Trends: NC Mulls Rewarding Colleges for Grad Rates." *Community College Week*, Dec. 1, 2010. Retrieved June 20, 2011, from http://www.ccweek.com/news/templates/template.aspx?articleid=2206&zoneid=3.

Barr, M. J., and Keating, L. A. "Introduction: Elements of Program Development." In M. J. Barr and L. A. Keating (eds.), *Developing Effective Student Services Programs.* San Francisco: Jossey-Bass, 1985.

Bureau of Labor Statistics. "Employment and Unemployment among Youth Summary." Washington, DC: U.S. Department of Labor. Retrieved June 20, 2011, from http://www.bls.gov/news.release/youth.nr0.htm, 2010.

Chickering, A. W., and Reisser, L. *Education and Identity* (2nd ed.). San Francisco: Jossey-Bass, 1993.

Cuyjet. M. J. "Program Development in Group Advising." In S. R. Komives and D. B. Woodard, Jr. (eds.), *Student Services: A Handbook for the Profession* (3rd ed.). San Francisco: Jossey-Bass, 1996.

Harris-Bowlsbey, J., Suddarth, B. H., and Reile, D. M. *Facilitating Career Development Student Development* (rev. 2nd ed.). Broken Arrow, OK: National Career Development Association, 2008.

Indiana Commission on Higher Education. "Transferin.net." Retrieved April 7, 2012, from www.transferin.net/index.aspx, 2012.

Koc, E. W. NACE Research. *NACE Journal*, February 2010.

Neugarten, B. L. "Time, Age, and the Life Cycle." *American Journal of Psychiatry, 136*(7), 1979.

Office of Postsecondary Education. "Federal TRIO Programs." Washington D.C.: U.S. Department of Education. Retrieved June 20, 2011, from http://www2.ed.gov/about/offices/list/ope/trio/index.html, 2011.

Office of Vocational and Adult Education. "Transferring from Community Colleges to Baccalaureate Institutions." Washington, DC: U.S. Department of Education. Retrieved June 20, 2011, from http://www2.ed.gov/about/offices/list/ovae/pi/cclo/transfer.html, 2008.

Palmer, J. C. "General Education in an Age of Student Mobility: What Do We Know about Student Transfer? An Overview." Washington, DC: Association of American Colleges and Universities. Retrieved June 20, 2011, from http://www.aacu.org/transfer/student_mobility/whatdoweknow.cfm, 2011.

Puente Project. Retrieved Feb. 2011 from http://www.puente.net/.

Ryan, J. R. *Lessons from Mom: A Tribute to Loving Wisdom.* Deerfield Beach, FL: Health Communications, 1996.

Schlossberg, N. K. *Counseling Adults in Transition.* New York: Springer, 1984.

United States Department of Education. "Ronald E. McNair Postbaccalaureate Achievement Program." Washington, DC. Retrieved June 20, 2011, from http://www2.ed.gov /programs/triomcnair/index.html, 2011.

United States Department of Labor. Fact Sheet #71: Internship Programs under the Fair Labor Standards Act. Washington, DC. Retrieved June 20, 2011, from http://www.dol .gov/whd/regs/compliance/whdfs71.htm, 2010.

Wiser, D. "UNC System Funding Scrutinized." *Daily Tar Heel*, December 3, 2010. Retrieved June 20, 2011, from http://www.dailytarheel.com/index.php/article /2010/12/uncsystem_funding_scrutinized.

Jim F. McAtee is director of Career Services at Indiana University–Purdue University Fort Wayne (IPFW).

New Directions for Student Services • DOI: 10.1002/ss

4

*This chapter describes four programs designed to assist
students in the transition to after-college life.*

Four Programmatic Approaches to Assisting Students' Transition from College

Amy Diepenbrock and Wanda Gibson

Transitioning from college can be a process in life that fills students with
trepidation. They may experience feelings of uncertainty and anxiety over
issues related to transferring to another college, going on to graduate
school, entering military service, or moving into the world of work. Recognizing that these topics may cause distress to their students, colleges
and universities can choose to address these concerns in programmatic
ways. This chapter presents four case studies describing programs that
were established to assist college students with their next steps after
college.

Barry University's Graduate School Awareness Week

Barry University is a comprehensive Catholic University in Miami Shores,
Florida. While offering more than one hundred undergraduate, graduate,
professional, and doctoral degrees, Barry offers a personal feel to education
with a student to faculty ratio of 14 : 1 (Barry University, 2009a). Degree
programs vary across the institution's nine schools and colleges: Frank J.
Rooney School of Adult and Continuing Education, College of Arts and
Sciences, College of Health Sciences (including the Division of Nursing),
Andreas School of Business, Adrian Dominican School of Education, School
of Human Performance and Leisure Sciences, Dwayne O. Andreas School
of Law, School of Podiatric Medicine, and Ellen Whiteside McDonnell
School of Social Work. Barry University's mission emphasizes knowledge
and truth, including a philosophy of "lifelong learning, growth, and development" (Barry University, 2009b). "Grounded in the liberal arts, it is not
surprising that roughly 12–15 percent of each graduating class continues

NEW DIRECTIONS FOR STUDENT SERVICES, no. 138, Summer 2012 © Wiley Periodicals, Inc.
Published online in Wiley Online Library (wileyonlinelibrary.com) • DOI: 10.1002/ss.20005

their education immediately by attending graduate school" (J. Moriarty, personal communication, September 1, 2010). Graduate School Awareness Week seeks to educate and prepare students for transition to graduate school with focuses on decision making, preparation, admission, and attendance.

The Idea. In the spring semester of 2007, the Career Services department, housed within the Division of Student Affairs, reorganized the structure of major events and career fairs. Until this point, both fall and spring career fairs were held each academic year. Graduate program representatives were invited to attend along with organizations and corporations looking to hire interns and full-time employees across all industries. To best prepare all students of all majors for life after college, the Career Services staff developed a new model with multiple industry-specific career fairs, including the first-ever Graduate School Information Fair. With over 35 programs represented from across Barry's campus, the state of Florida, and the East Coast of the United States, this event proved to be a successful way to expose students to graduate school opportunities. Over the next three years, the Graduate School Information Fair grew into Graduate School Awareness Week with a focus on informing students not only about the wide variety of opportunities available for graduate education, but also about preparing for the application and admissions process as well as becoming a graduate student.

Development of the Program. In 2008, Graduate School Awareness Week began with a facts campaign across campus. On day one, signs were placed in strategic high-traffic areas on campus with facts about the application process and admissions statistics for graduate, medical, and law school. The Graduate School Information Fair was held on day two, featuring both programs within the schools and colleges on Barry's campus as well as programs throughout the state of Florida. Lecture-style workshops throughout the week focused on educating students on the decision process as to whether to go to graduate school, what students can do if they take a year off before attending, and financing options for graduate school. The week concluded with test preparation sessions during which students could take 15-minute versions of the GRE and LSAT entrance exams and receive immediate feedback and study tips.

In 2009, the Graduate School Information Fair remained as it was during the week, but all other activities were adjusted. Instead of a temporary awareness campaign with signs across campus, the staff developed a *Graduate School Guidebook* as a supplement to the *Career Guide* produced annually by the Center. The week started with a launch that included free food, the debut of the *Graduate School Guidebook* as a giveaway, and information about the week's events. A panel format was utilized for the session on financing graduate school. Panelists included a research assistant, administrative graduate assistant, teaching assistant, and a student employed full time with tuition reimbursement. Test preparation was expanded to include the full versions of the MCAT and GMAT practice tests exams, along with abbreviated versions of the GRE and LSAT.

The 2010 Graduate School Awareness Week began with a launch similar to that in 2009. Because of the small number of attendees at workshops and panels, the staff decided to utilize high attendance at the Graduate School Information Fair to create awareness of the decision-making process and financing options for graduate school. During the 2010 fair, Career Services staff hosted tables throughout the event with information regarding such topics. Lastly, the test preparation sessions during the 2010 event included full versions of the GRE, LSAT, and MCAT practice tests.

Responsibility and Budget. Graduate School Awareness Week at Barry University is sponsored by the department of Career Services. The Senior Director of Graduate Admissions and staff within the Financial Aid office are strategic partners for collaboration. Both areas have assisted in presenting workshops in past years and also in posting the fair information to the National Association of Graduate Admissions Professionals (NAGAP) to promote attendance by external programs.

Graduate School Awareness Week is a low-cost event. Printing of the *Graduate School Guidebook* costs approximately $1,000, and the guides are used throughout this week of events as well as throughout the year. The cost of tables for the Graduate School Information Fair and providing lunch for representatives at this event constitute the majority of the expenses and depend on the number of program representatives attending. The cost of lunch per organization at the fair is around $20 for two representatives. Programs not associated with the university pay a registration fee of $100, which covers these costs and assists with funding the guidebooks as well. Barry University graduate programs are invited to participate in the fair but they do not pay a registration fee. The kickoff event includes complimentary coffee and donuts. The cost for this portion of the week is less than $200. Test preparation sessions are sponsored by Kaplan Test Prep and therefore are free to Career Services and student participants.

The Career Services budget supports Graduate School Awareness Week with $1,500 allocated for the weeklong series of events. As stated above, the cost varies depending on the number of participating organizations at the fair. Additional expenses are paid through revenue generated with registration fees. This event can produce revenue beyond the cost of the events, again depending on participation.

Program Goals and Assessment. Graduate School Awareness Week was developed with four goals. It was intended that students who attend events throughout this week would:

- Be exposed to graduate school options
- Be able to explain what is expected of graduate and professional school applicants

New Directions for Student Services • DOI: 10.1002/ss

- Be able to describe the different options for financing graduate school
- Have increased confidence regarding the decision to attend graduate school

At the end of the week, students who attended one or more of the week's events are sent a link to an online survey. Self-reported data are collected to assess the effectiveness of the week's program. A free online survey tool has been utilized to collect such information, yet response rates have not been high enough to have useful data to disseminate. Given the open space locations utilized for many of the events throughout this week, it is difficult to collect assessment data as participants exit each session or event. Planning for future Graduate School Awareness Week programs would benefit from a more efficient way to collect data.

DeSales University's Senior Success Series

DeSales University, formerly Allentown College, is a small Catholic institution located in central Pennsylvania. With a student to faculty ratio of 15:1 and an average class size of 18 students, this institution of roughly 1,500 traditional, daytime undergraduate students offers a variety of degrees (DeSales University, 2010b). Degree programs are largely focused on the liberal arts and sciences but also include disciplines such as health and education (DeSales University, 2010a). Regardless of major or degree, the Division of Student Life at DeSales works to "promote a total campus environment that fosters the academic, spiritual, social, and moral development of each student" (DeSales University, 2010d). The Senior Success Series, founded in 2007, brings to life this philosophy as it strategically prepares its outgoing students in their senior year for life after college.

The Idea. As a small liberal arts institution, DeSales has traditionally focused on majors and academics, and the Senior Success Series was developed to address the transitional issues seniors face as they leave the institution (J. P. Kelliher, personal communication, July 28, 2010). In Spring 2007, staff from Residence Life, Career Services and Internships, and Academic Advising came together to discuss collaborative ways to assist students in transitioning to life after college. The group sought to find a way in which to reduce the gap between the academic side and practical life skills training side of higher education. Students were well educated and possessed the critical thinking, problem solving, and other skills that liberal arts students gain throughout college. Yet the institution did not have specific programs that intentionally prepared the students for after-college life. The Senior Success Series was created to expose students to the world beyond the classroom.

Development Phase. To ensure success of the program, the 2007–2008 year was utilized to collect research on similar programs and to survey current DeSales students and alumni on what was most important to them regarding post-college life. The first survey, which was completed by sixty seniors, stated that the topics most important to them were:

- Obtaining a job
- Student loans and debt
- Renting or buying housing
- Getting into graduate school
- Budgeting

A separate alumni survey completed by 147 people identified the following similar, but not identical, priorities:

- Obtaining a job
- Student loans and debt
- Budgeting
- Resume writing
- Job interviews

For both populations, obtaining a job was ranked as most important. From these results, a program to combine professional development opportunities with personal growth, character development, and civic responsibility was drafted to pair together the professional and personal needs of the graduating seniors in a cohesive structure.

As previously stated, the Senior Success Series is a collaborative effort among Residence Life, Career Services and Internships, and Academic Advising. Both Career Services and Internships and Academic Advising are housed in Academic Affairs, while Residence Life is housed in the Division of Student Life. Hence, the collaborative effort in support of this program required greater effort. According to J. P. Kelliher, Associate Director for Residence Life, "it was a year-long process of reviewing drafts to get the proposal accepted by both sides of the institution" (personal communication, July 28, 2010). The program was designed to bookend the existing First Year Experience program, referred to as Character U. Since Character U was required of all first-year students, the hope was to create a senior-level program that would eventually also be required for graduation. The accepted proposal was written with a student-life feel in academic language and included outcomes-based learning activities and assessment methods.

Budget and Responsibility. While the Senior Success Series was developed, proposed, and implemented as a collaborative effort among departments, it had to be housed somewhere. Career Services and Internships holds coordinating responsibility for the program. The initial proposal requested funding to be managed by the Director of Career Services in the form of a new line item for the Senior Success Series within the existing Career Services budget. Requested monies were allocated to books and workbooks for participants, materials and supplies for sessions, off-site travel, gifts for off-site travel hosts and presenters of sessions, and networking receptions.

The proposed budget for 2008–2009 totaled approximately $7,000 for an initial group of twenty-five students. The proposal was developed with the plan for participation to increase from 25 students in 2008–2009 to 400 students in 2012–2013. A 4 percent increase in costs per year for each of the first four years of the program was estimated in the initial program proposal. Finally, a part-time staff member was proposed to begin in the 2010–2011 year. With the increase in operational costs combined with the part-time staff salary, the proposed budget for the 2012–2013 academic year totaled $66,000. Upon approval of the proposal, money was sought and received during the annual budget planning process to allocate for this program in the Career Services and Internships budget. To offset costs, sponsors are routinely sought for networking events and closing banquets.

The Program. The Senior Success Series includes an introductory session, eight monthly sessions, and a closing banquet for participants. Selected students participate in the eight sessions, which address the topics noted in Table 4.1.

Table 4.1 Topics for Monthly Sessions

Networking	Teaches participants the details associated with professional networking
Creating a Brand	Teaches effective ways to identify and develop a core identity of values, experiences, and attributes to market for personal and professional benefit
Job Search	Helps participants become successful at locating employment opportunities that match their goals and ideals.
Personal/Professional Character	Incorporates activities related to conflict resolution, diversity, and maintaining congruency between values and actions
Interviewing	Teaches and allows for practice of effective interviewing techniques
What's Next	Exposes participants to office environments by discussing company culture, employee benefit options, and human resource policies and procedures
Finances	Promotes personal responsibility for creating a budget and managing finances
Community Engagement	Promotes social responsibility and suggests ways to get involved in the community

NEW DIRECTIONS FOR STUDENT SERVICES • DOI: 10.1002/ss

During the initial year of the program, the majority of sessions were conducted by staff in Residential Life, Career Services and Internships, and Academic Advising. The long-term goal, however, is to have staff facilitating the sessions while employers and community members give presentations. Progress toward the goal was made in the program's second year: Roughly one third of the presentations were conducted by internal staff in 2009–2010, while consultants, recruiters, or alumni presented topics such as job searches, interview skills, and finances. As the program moves forward, the goal will be to secure 100 percent external presenters (J.P. Kelliher, personal communication, July 28, 2010).

A unique aspect of the DeSales Senior Success Series is the application process. Students must complete an application that includes four essay questions (DeSales, 2010c). Applicants are asked to reflect on their current leadership activities, short- and long-term goals, concerns about life after graduation, and how the program will benefit them if selected. Two letters of recommendation must also be secured by applicants. According to Kelliher, "we select students who would both benefit from and contribute to the sessions and overall program" (personal communication, July 28, 2010). In addition to the application materials, the student's record of leadership and overall GPA are reviewed by a committee of faculty and staff from across campus.

Twenty students went through the Senior Success Series in its inaugural year. The second class, 2009–2010, expanded to forty-four students, thereby meeting the goal of increasing participation by 100 percent. For 2010–2011, the process was delayed due to a transition of staff in Career Services.

Program Goals and Assessment. The goals of this program include increased alumni satisfaction, an engaged community surrounding the campus, and enhanced marketability of the University for prospective students and parents. Directly observable assessment methods are utilized such as a business card designed by the student, a personal mission statement to market one's character, a professional resume and cover letter, and participation in mock interviews. Indirect assessment methods such as surveys from employer participants at networking events and facilitated group discussions are also used.

A pre-post test is utilized to measure the anxiety and stress of participants regarding life after college. Initial results from 2008–2009 showed an overall increase in students' perception of their preparation for graduate school or work upon graduation. The series seems to have been an effective way to prepare DeSales graduating seniors, as indicated in Table 4.2.

The plan is to develop additional assessment methods to determine how the Senior Success Series is affecting students over the first five years after graduation. Are students getting jobs, being promoted, receiving an increase in salary, and giving back to the community and university? These

NEW DIRECTIONS FOR STUDENT SERVICES • DOI: 10.1002/ss

Table 4.2 Perceived Preparation for Graduate School or Work upon Graduation Pre/Post Test Results

Item	Pre-Test	Post-Test
Reported having a strategy that makes them feel more confident about their ability to succeed personally and professionally after graduation	61.91% Strongly or Somewhat Agree	93.75% Strongly or Somewhat Agree
Had a resume reviewed by a career counselor	50% Yes	93.75% Yes
Completed a mock interview	72.73% Yes	100% Yes
Expressed confidence that if they were asked to interview for a job for which they believed they were qualified, they would be offered the job	40.91% Completely or Very Confident	81.25% Completely or Very Confident
Stated that if asked to complete a tax form on their first day of work, they could successfully do this task	45.45% Yes	87.50% Yes

questions will take time to answer but are important to the continuous development of the program.

The University of Georgia's Career Academy

The University of Georgia (UGA) is a large, public university located in Athens, Georgia. Its student population is nearly 35,000, including over 26,000 undergraduates. The University's Career Center, a part of the Division of External Affairs, is open to all students but primarily serves undergraduates. The Career Center's Career Academy is a one-day program that prepares undergraduates for the world of work. Beginning in 2005, the original targeted audience for the program was juniors and seniors. While upperclassmen are still the targeted audience, the program has been opened to underclassmen as the belief is that it is never too early to expose students to such preparedness.

The Idea. The idea for the Career Academy grew out of the Career Center's desire to help juniors and seniors get ready for life after college and to prepare them for the job search. The staff wanted to create an intensive one-day conference that would help students launch their job search, a critical part of which is exposure to employers. Through the vision of combining job search skill development and employer contact, the Career Academy was developed. Approximately 150–200 students register for

NEW DIRECTIONS FOR STUDENT SERVICES • DOI: 10.1002/ss

Career Academy each year and take advantage of this on-campus opportunity (M. Higgins, personal communication, August 23, 2010).

The Program. The Career Academy is an annual event that occurs before fall classes begin. Participants are exposed to such topics as what employers look for in candidates, how to network, the development of a resume, interviewing skills, business etiquette (including dining and professionalism), relocation/adjustment issues, and what to expect during the first year on the job. Students preregister for the event and pay a small registration fee.

The program consists of an entire day of activities. After the morning check-in, there is a welcome by the Career Center Executive Director and then the morning plenary sessions begin. The plenary sessions range in length from one hour to an hour and fifteen minutes, depending on the topic. The first session is a varied panel of employers, facilitated by the Executive Director, on what employers are looking for in employees. Each employer is able to give a description of the types of candidates that would be the best fit for their organization. General information is also disseminated about how to be the best candidate for any type of position. Students are able to ask questions of the employers during this panel discussion. Additional plenary sessions on selected topics are offered in the morning before the break for lunch.

Following lunch, students choose the sessions they want to attend. There are three topic options that run concurrently in two afternoon sessions for a total of six different topics covered. The breakout sessions are facilitated jointly by the Career Center staff and employers and are traditionally more lecture-style with some interactive components. Additionally, because a major goal of the Career Academy is to expose students to employers, during the course of the day the participants also attend an interactive networking fair to meet the employers on an individual level. Table 4.3 shows a sample schedule for the day of events (M. Higgins, personal communication, August 23, 2010).

Budget and Responsibility. The Career Academy is exclusively the responsibility of the UGA Career Center. In the late spring or early summer of each year, a committee convenes to plan the upcoming fall's program agenda. Each year, the program agenda is set based upon relevant topics at the time.

Funding for the program originally came from a grant the Career Center received from a single corporate sponsor. In subsequent years, the Career Academy has been funded through obtaining multiple corporate sponsorships. The Career Center offers corporate organizations the opportunity to annually sponsor various programs within their office; the Career Academy is one of those opportunities. In exchange for sponsorship, these organizations are given the chance to have a table at the Career Academy, co-present one of the sessions with UGA Career Center staff members, and participate in the networking event to meet students. Furthermore, the

Table 4.3 Sample Career Academy Schedule

Time	Event
8:00 A.M.	Registration and Continental Breakfast
8:30 A.M.	Welcome
8:45 A.M.	What Employers Really Want Presented by Employer Panel—Facilitated by Career Center Staff
9:45 A.M.	Break
10:00 A.M.–11:10 A.M.	Leveraging Social Media Presented by Career Center Staff
11:15 A.M.–1:00 P.M.	Business Lunch—Etiquette and Professional Style Presented by Etiquette Consultant
1:15 P.M.–2:15 P.M.	Networking Fair
2:15 P.M.	Break
2:30 P.M.–3:30 P.M.	Breakout Sessions: It's Your Resume, Get It Right! Presented by Career Center Staff and Employer Developing Your Network Presented by Career Center Staff and Employer How to Work a Career Fair Presented by Career Center Staff and Employer
3:30 P.M.–4:30 P.M.	Breakout Sessions: Alternative Career Choices Presented by Career Center Staff and Employer Developing Your Job Search Campaign Presented by Career Center Staff and Employer Transitions … First Year on the Job Presented by Career Center Staff and Employer
4:30 P.M.	Closing Remarks

student participants are charged a small fee. Funded through the registration fees and corporate sponsorship, the students receive a padfolio and pen to assist them with their professional appearance as they begin their job search process (M. Higgins, personal communication, August 23, 2010).

Program Goals and Assessment. The overarching goals of the Career Academy are to give participants a crash course in developing job search skills and expose them to employers early. At the conclusion of the program, participants are sent an evaluation along with a link to a website that houses the PowerPoint presentations of the sessions. At this point, learning

NEW DIRECTIONS FOR STUDENT SERVICES • DOI: 10.1002/ss

outcomes are not measured. This may be incorporated into future programs. However, satisfaction is measured as the students are asked how they heard about the program, to rate the sessions they attended, what they liked about Career Academy, and to offer suggestions for improvement. The Career Center staff also receives feedback from the employers who attend the event. This information is then used to inform the planning committee for the next year's Career Academy (M. Higgins, personal communication, August 23, 2010).

University of Florida Opportunity Scholars and the Academy of Leadership Programs

The University of Florida is a large, comprehensive university located in Gainesville, Florida. The university has more than 50,000 graduate and undergraduate students and is one of the largest institutions of higher learning in the United States (University of Florida, 2010a). With a commitment to providing access for all qualified students, the university embarked on an initiative that would assist a population of students who might find it difficult to achieve their dreams of a college education.

The University of Florida's Opportunity Scholars (FOS) program provides low socioeconomic, first-generation students with the necessary tools for success in college. It is both a scholarship and a support program. Started in 2006, this program offers funding in the form of scholarships and grants for first-time, first-generation students to help them meet the cost of their education without incurring the financial burden that these students can often face. Not only is financial support provided for the students in the FOS program, but other support services such as academic advising, group support counseling, mentoring, and social activities are also offered from various areas around the campus. In order to be eligible for this program, a student must meet certain financial and residential requirements: have a family income of $40,000 or less, be a first-generation college student, be a Florida resident, and be enrolling in college for the first time—this program does not admit transfer students. There are approximately 1,400 students in the FOS program (L. Pendleton, personal communication, March 15, 2011).

A goal of the FOS program is not only to get students to college, but to help them graduate and successfully transition to life after college. As participants in the program, students must continue to meet financial requirements, be enrolled full time, maintain a 2.0 grade point average, earn 24 credit hours each year, and attend freshman year seminars on financial literacy and sophomore year seminars on career development to remain eligible. They may receive the funding for up to eight semesters of enrollment at the University of Florida. The program also requires that students participate in a peer mentor program and enroll in First Year Florida, a course dedicated to acclimating students to the academic and social adjustments and resources of college during their freshman year (University of Florida 2010b).

The Florida Opportunity Scholars program initially was more heavily focused on the first and second years of college. Limited programming existed to connect juniors and seniors to the FOS program. Knowing that the provision of financial and on-campus support services to get students to graduation is only part of the picture of success, the institution searched for a solution to meet student needs for transitioning out of college. Students can graduate without the knowledge or tools necessary for navigating the world of work and the soft skills necessary for career success. This can be much more of an issue with first-generation students. The Florida Opportunity Scholars Academy of Leadership was created to address these transitioning concerns for the participants.

The Idea. The Florida Opportunity Scholars Academy of Leadership (FOSAL) is a program within the Florida Opportunity Scholars program. FOSAL focuses on aspects of the FOS program that were not a part of the original idea, with an emphasis on connecting junior and senior students to the parent program. It provides leadership development—a valued skill for one's career development. The program aims to attract those students who are not as connected in areas of leadership as some of their peers. The Academy of Leadership also prepares students for life after college and offers adult mentorship to assist them with the transition process. There are four outcomes identified for the program: leadership understanding, self-awareness, career preparation, and global citizenship (L. Pendleton, personal communication, March 15, 2011).

The Program. The Florida Opportunity Scholars program has undergone changes based upon evaluation of the program and its needs. One of those changes was to add a director. There needed to be someone to specifically have oversight of the entire Florida Opportunity Scholars program, continuing the vision and enhancing it. The director came on board in August 2009. One immediate enhancement to the program was the FOSAL component of FOS, added in January 2010.

Entrance to the FOSAL program is limited and students are chosen through an application process. Fifty junior and senior students are chosen to participate (L. Pendleton, personal communication, March 15, 2011). Applicants must meet a 2.5 GPA requirement to be eligible, which is higher than the GPA required to remain in the overall FOS program. The application includes letters of recommendation as well as several reflection essays. As the program starts in January, the applications are due in November and selection is made shortly thereafter (L. Pendleton, personal communication, May 10, 2011).

After the selection process, the Academy of Leadership begins in January and runs through November. It is a three-part program comprised of spring, summer, and fall activities. During the spring semester, there is a kickoff retreat that introduces the program to students to let them know what they can expect. Also during the spring, students are required to participate in three experiences. These are experiences that the students choose and can range from networking, visiting a local organization or business of interest to learn about that particular work environment, participating in etiquette dinners, or conducting a service project. These experiences do not have to be hands-on, but they must provide students with useful career information. During the summer, the students are required to participate in another experience, but this time it must be one where they are able to actually fully engage in the experience and not merely be an observer. Examples of the applied experience are a summer internship or an extensive volunteer opportunity. Students must also journal about their experience as a tool of reflection. When the students return in the fall, they participate in a symposium where they are able to tell other FOSAL participants of their summer experience. They must also complete three additional experiences such as the ones required in the spring semester. The formal program culminates with a banquet for the students (L. Pendleton, personal communication, March 15, 2011).

Budget and Responsibility. In 2005, the vice president for Student Affairs was given the responsibility by the president of the University of Florida to create the FOS program with its financial component for scholarship support. Therefore, the Florida Opportunity Scholars program is housed in the Division of Student Affairs. While the program is within Student Affairs and many of the services and collaborators are in the Division as well, the program stretches across other divisions to create support services for the participants. For example, Academic Advising is another support service that works with FOS.

The overall program is funded by donations through the University of Florida Foundation. Additionally, the Florida legislature has set aside funding through the First Generation Matching Grant Program (University of Florida, 2010b). Initially, the FOSAL program was given additional funding by the president of the university because it is of great importance to the university. This funding covers expenses such as the annual overnight Professional Leadership Retreat, the annual Symposium where students talk about their summer experience, the final banquet, and purchasing assessments (L. Pendleton, personal communication, March 15, 2011).

Program Goals and Assessment. The goal of the FOSAL is to help students acquire valuable skills to assist them with transitioning out of college. The achievement of the outcomes identified for the program (leadership understanding, self-awareness, career preparation, and global citizenship) is facilitated through a variety of avenues. Two of these avenues include taking assessments (StrengthsQuest and MBTI) or participating in the offerings of the Career Resource Center. Students are given a pre- and post-test to see how the program influenced them in the four areas. The results from the 2010 FOSAL participants can be seen in Table 4.4 (L. Pendleton, personal communication, March 15, 2011).

Table 4.4 Pre/Post Assessment of Learning Outcomes

Item	Pre-Test*	Post-Test*
Leadership Understanding: I understand basic leadership principles.	62.5%	90%
Leadership Understanding: I understand the meaning of leadership.	63.27%	87.1%
Self-Awareness: I am aware of my strengths.	67.34%	90.32%
Self-Awareness: I am confident in my leadership abilities.	45.84%	93.34%
Career Preparation: I know how to prepare for an interview.	35.42%	70%
Career Preparation: I have a mentor with whom I discuss my career plans.	20.83%	51.61%
Global Citizenship: I understand how I will apply global leadership principles in my career.	43.75%	80.64%
Global Citizenship: I understand how my decisions contribute to the larger global society.	47.92%	87.1%

*Percent of FOSAL Students who responded either good or exceptional for these areas (Pendleton, 2011).

The results show increasing student knowledge in the program's four key areas believed to aid in student success after college. While the FOSAL program is fairly new in its creation, having completed one full cycle of participants at this point, the program does show promise. The program will continue to be evaluated and with continued success, perhaps expanded to provide even more resources to assist students with their transition out of college.

Conclusion

Students go to college to be better prepared for the next stage of their lives. Sometimes students leave college with uncertainty about how to approach that next stage. A consistent thread throughout the Barry, DeSales, University of Georgia, and University of Florida case studies is that an important goal for each program is the preparation for life after college. Graduate school knowledge, professional development, and job search readiness are all important factors in this process.

Programs that address these kinds of student concerns should become commonplace so that students not only leave college with broadened academic knowledge, but they leave ready to take full advantage of what the future offers them. In addition to the programmatic approach, it is critical for curriculum to also address the transition to life after college. Chapter Five offers an overview of curricular approaches for student affairs professionals and faculty who work with students during this transition.

References

Barry University. "About Barry." Retrieved Sept. 1, 2010, from http://www.barry.edu/aboutbarry/default.htm, 2009a.

Barry University. "Mission Statement and Core Commitments." Retrieved Sept. 1, 2010, from http://www.barry.edu/aboutbarry/mission.htm, 2009b.

DeSales University. "Divisions and Majors." Retrieved July 30, 2010, from http://desales.edu/default.aspx?pageid=17, 2010a.

DeSales University. "Facts and Figures." Retrieved July 30, 2010, from http://desales.edu/default.aspx?pageid=11, 2010b.

DeSales University. "Senior Success Series Application." Retrieved July 30, 2010, from http://www.desales.edu/assets/desales/CareerServ/2010-2011_Application_%282%29.pdf, 2010c.

DeSales University. "Student Affairs Offices." Retrieved July 30, 2010, from http://desales.edu/default.aspx?pageid=1346, 2010d.

Pendleton, L. "Transition-Out Programming for First-Generation College Students." Presented at the Annual NASPA conference. Philadelphia, PA, 2011.

University of Florida. "About the University of Florida." Retrieved April 29, 2011 from http://www.ufl.edu/aboutUF/, 2010a.

University of Florida. "Fall 2008–2009: Full Annual Report." Retrieved April 29, 2011, from http://fos.ufsa.ufl.edu/doc/FOS%2008-09%20Annual%20Rpt%20FINAL.pdf, 2010b.

AMY DIEPENBROCK is the director of the Civic Engagement and Career Development Center at St. Mary's University in San Antonio, Texas.

WANDA GIBSON is the associate director of Career Counseling and Programs in the Career Development Office at Pomona College in Claremont, California.

5

Institutions use both programmatic and curricular approaches to address students' transition to life after college. While Chapter Four discusses the programmatic approaches, this chapter provides an overview of the curricular approaches.

Overview of Curricular Approaches

Cameo V. Hartz and Jill Parker

Institutions of higher education address the transition from after-college life in a variety of curricular approaches. Articulation agreements provide greater transferability of courses from one college to another, thereby easing the transition for students. Career courses, which are typically taught by career center staff, are a common offering to students at any time during their college careers. These can be general in nature or major- or program-specific. There are also capstone courses, which are offered toward the end of a student's degree. Such courses can serve multiple purposes, including serving as an indicator to faculty of the quality of their program through a final project; providing a method of assessing the institution's programs and whether student learning and program outcomes have been met; and addressing students' transition to the world beyond, whether it is to further education or to work. Additionally, internships for credit are handled in the context of a course, whether it is through a for-credit internship course or a general independent study course. This chapter explores each of these options and in doing so draws on examples from various types of institutions. The intent is that student affairs practitioners and faculty alike will draw inspiration and practical knowledge just as readily from dissimilar organizations as those that are similar in profile.

Articulation Agreements

One curricular approach that is often overlooked, yet is essential in easing the transition of students from one college to the next, especially from a two-year to four-year institution, is articulation agreements. United States Code, Title 20 (2010) defines an articulation agreement as "an agreement

New Directions for Student Services, no. 138, Summer 2012 © Wiley Periodicals, Inc.
Published online in Wiley Online Library (wileyonlinelibrary.com) • DOI: 10.1002/ss.20006

between or among institutions of higher education that specifies the accept-ability of courses in transfer toward meeting specific degree or program requirements." A more inclusive definition of articulation agreement can be found in the "Creating an Articulation Agreement" booklet developed by the Kansas State Department of Education:

> A written commitment (A) that is agreed upon at the state level or approved annually by the lead administrators of (1) a secondary school and a college; or (2) a postsecondary associate degree granting institution and a baccalaure-ate degree granting institution; and (B) a program (1) designed to provide students with a nonduplicative sequence of progressive achievement leading to a technical skill proficiency, a credential, a certificate or a degree; and (2) linked through credit transfer agreements between the institutions. (Kansas State Department of Education, n.d.)

Articulation agreements exist as a formal way to help students make a seamless transition between one institution of higher education and another, if not more than one. Students can utilize them to make informed choices about the classes they take, thereby addressing the recent trend of consumerism in higher education. If students want more for their money and parents and guardians want to ensure their students are taking only the classes they need to transfer, the articulation agreement provides an ideal opportunity for all involved to get the most education for their investment.

Additionally, articulation agreements inform student affairs practitio-ners and faculty. For example, academic advisors provide information about the classes students need to transfer from one college to another. Articulation agreements are also helpful to admissions staff and department faculty to aid them in the evaluation of transfer credit. On an outcome-oriented level, they allow faculty and administration to gauge the useful-ness of their programs and the rigor of their classes. If one college refuses to accept the coursework of another based on poor course quality or prepa-ration for higher-level classes, it can lead to faculty and administration assessing their courses and programs to determine the cause.

There are a variety of types of articulation agreements. Articulation agreements exist most commonly between two-year and four-year institu-tions, especially four-year public colleges and universities. However, they also are created for two or more private institutions, two or more private and public colleges, consortia, colleges at the system level, and even public high schools and community colleges when college-level tech prep courses are taken at the high school (for example, the Kern/South Tulare Consor-tium in California) (Bakersfield College, 2006).

An example of an articulation agreement among a consortium is Vir-ginia Tidewater Consortium, which consists of "four community colleges, four public colleges and universities, four private colleges, and a National

Defense University" (Virginia Tidewater Consortium for Higher Education, 2008). The articulation agreement allows courses taken as part of the AA and AS degrees to satisfy the lower-division course requirements at the four-year public and private institutions.

The North Carolina Comprehensive Articulation Agreement between the University of North Carolina and the North Carolina Community College System (NCCCS) is an example of a system-level model. The University of North Carolina's website describes the various elements of the agreement and provides additional resources that may be helpful to students and others in understanding and making use of the agreement. The elements and resources listed include:

- Manual containing the Associate of Arts (AA), Science (AS), and Fine Arts (AFA) articulation agreements
- List of the transfer courses accepted at both UNC and NCCCS
- Transfer guides with frequently asked questions
- Listing of the independent colleges/universities that also endorse the Comprehensive Articulation Agreement
- Contact information for the members of the Transfer Advisory Board
- Transfer Advisory Board meeting minutes (University of North Carolina, n.d.)

This is an example of an effort to make the process of creating and updating articulation agreements transparent and accessible to the public at large.

The Indiana Core Transfer Library (CTL) is a model of a statewide agreement. The CTL comprises "a list of courses that will transfer among all Indiana public college and university campuses, assuming adequate grades. All Core Transfer Library courses will meet the general education or free elective requirements of undergraduate degree programs" (Indiana Commission for Higher Education, n.d.). Students can view a list of CTL courses by course name or by institution, which helps them to see how their courses will transfer. Advisors and counselors can also utilize the website to view course transferability, research the policies on dual credit, and provide information on military transcripts to student veterans. Additional work is presently under way to determine equivalent courses between public and independent colleges in Indiana (Indiana Commission for Higher Education, n.d.).

Having discussed various models of articulation agreements, it is important to note that such agreements offer both strengths and challenges. An obvious strength is a more seamless transition for students. Additionally, students can benefit from seeing early on in their college career how their entry-level coursework will count toward a more advanced degree, which can certainly have a positive effect on retention. However, while articulation agreements between individual colleges allow for more unique and appropriate institutional relationships, they can create confusion for advisors and students alike with the articulation agreement language differing from college to college. Conversely, system-wide articulation agreements remove the problems with language, but to obtain uniformity, the relationships between colleges and departments can be sacrificed. One overarching articulation agreement can be designed with the intention of being inclusive of more colleges, but it makes it difficult for all institutions to follow that agreement.

An important consideration for colleges creating articulation agreements is how policies around the agreements will affect all students. For example, colleges that choose to not accept credit for prior learning (for example, the College Level Examination Program credit) can seriously affect nontraditional students who may wish to bypass certain requirements in order to accelerate their graduation. Also, students with disabilities who cannot complete a public speaking course may request a course substitution to satisfy degree requirements. Because some colleges do not allow course substitutions as part of articulation agreements, students may unknowingly preclude themselves from being eligible for coverage under the agreement. This brings to light the challenges faced by nontraditional students or special populations regarding articulation agreements that are often geared toward traditional students.

In addition, degree-granting institutions sometimes fail to fully honor existing articulation agreements. This failure is commonly the result of an individual or department developing an interpretation or decision independent of a broader institutional review. Failure to honor an articulation agreement can leave students feeling as though their trust in the institutions has been betrayed and thus seek an advocate or avenue of redress. Finding themselves in this position, students may seek the assistance of a trusted student affairs professional or faculty member or simply bring their complaint to the appropriate oversight body. In an era when completion of degrees is of utmost importance to institutions of higher education, not to mention the U.S. government, an articulation agreement that is not honored by the institution accepting the transfer can have devastating effects on its reputation, and thus its transfer and retention rates.

Career Courses

In this section, career courses in a variety of forms will be addressed. The prevalence of such courses will be discussed, as will their impact and availability, outcomes, and variations in design.

Prevalence. Findings from research on the prevalence of career courses on college campuses can vary depending on the institutions involved in surveys. Two broad sample surveys had similar findings, whereas the survey conducted of the members of the National Association of Colleges and Employers (NACE) produced different findings.

NEW DIRECTIONS FOR STUDENT SERVICES • DOI: 10.1002/ss

Broad sample surveys. Folsom, Reardon, and Lee (2005) provided a synthesis of historical trends in career courses by decade, with the bulk of the literature they reviewed published between 1976 and 2005. Included in that synthesis was a national survey conducted by Mead and Korschgen (as cited in Folsom et al., 2005) of 61 colleges from 32 states, which found that 62 percent offered a career course. These courses fell into three categories: career decision-making courses, job-search preparation courses, and courses geared toward specific disciplines. "Ninety-five percent of the respondents granted from one to three hours of credit, and 5 percent of the courses were graded pass/fail" (p. 5).

A national study conducted by Halasz and Kempton found that 28 of 40 responding colleges offered a career course, typically for one credit. A notable finding in this survey was "that the presence or absence of administrative and faculty support was a key issue in offering a career course" (as cited in Folsom et al., 2005, p. 5).

NACE surveys. In contrast to the responses found in the national surveys, NACE, a professional organization with membership from colleges, universities, and employers with interest in college recruiting, reported in its 2009–2010 Career Services Benchmark Survey for Four-Year Colleges and Universities that just under one third of 557 participating respondents offer a career course for credit (NACE, 2010b). Collins "found that credit-bearing courses were offered by 30 percent of those responding, a figure that has held steady since 1981, while 24 percent offered noncredit-bearing courses" (as cited in Folsom et al., 2005, p. 5).

Impact and Availability. Whiston, Sexton, and Lazoff (as cited in Folsom et al., 2005) conducted a survey of the types of interventions offered by career services office, and their findings indicated that

> career classes were the third most effective career intervention out of eight different categories of interventions examined. Career classes followed individual and group counseling in effectiveness, but were ahead of group test interpretation, workshops, computer interventions, counselor-free interventions, and other nonclassified interventions (p. 7).

Furthermore, the availability of credit-bearing courses offered by career centers can also be compared to the prevalence of other services by using the 2009–2010 NACE data for career centers at both two-year and four-year institutions. The data across a variety of sources indicate that there are several types of career-related services that are virtually universal on college campuses. Career courses, however, are not among the universal offerings. In fact, they rank low in frequency on campuses when compared against other services. Considering whether a career course is a viable approach is a decision many career centers have to weigh carefully in times of limited resources and competing demands, consumerism in higher

NEW DIRECTIONS FOR STUDENT SERVICES • DOI: 10.1002/ss

education, results-based funding, and emphasis (and some argue overemphasis) on placement rates.

Two-Year Colleges. The NACE 2009 Career Services Benchmark Survey for Two-Year Colleges is a report specific to two-year colleges that includes comparative data about services offered. The report indicated that over 40 percent of career services offices at institutions that responded to the survey offer career classes and that 45.9 percent of them host career classes offered by an "office other than career services" (NACE, 2009, p. 10).

The services offered most commonly at career centers at two-year colleges included class presentations (100 percent), career outreach (98.9 percent), career advising by appointment (97.8 percent), and alumni services (93.5 percent). Academic counseling in all situations (by appointment, 37.9 percent; drop-in, 28.7 percent; and online, 16.5 percent) was offered less often than career courses by career centers at two-year colleges (NACE, 2009, p. 7).

Four-Year Colleges and Universities. NACE also conducts a benchmarking survey for four-year colleges and universities. Patterns in the data were very similar to the findings for the two-year colleges. Analysis of the 2009–2010 NACE (2010b) data revealed "... that the relationship between providing career classes and size of school is directly reversed—the smaller the school, the less likely that career services will be providing career classes for credit" (p. 12).

By acknowledging the uniqueness of the curricular approach within the range of possible career services, the creators, instructors, and collaborators involved in career courses have an enhanced opportunity to engage directly with campus-specific programmatic and student needs. As may be expected, many efforts also require rich and ongoing commitment that includes high expectations for associated programmatic and learning outcomes. The curricular descriptions offered later in this chapter, as well as the case studies presented in Chapter Six, highlight aspects of collaboration across and beyond campus, cohesiveness and depth of content, and other benefits.

Learning Outcomes. While it is easy to point to the amount of variation in career courses, Folsom et al. provide a cohesive summary of their meta-analysis of studies. They state that

> there is overwhelming evidence that career courses have a positive impact on the cognitive functioning of students, and these courses also appear to have a positive impact on student outcomes, including satisfaction with career courses and increased retention in college. Only 4 of the 40 studies involving career course outputs failed to show a positive impact of a career course, while 90% of the studies we reviewed showed positive gains in vocational identity, career decision making, or other output variables. Similarly, of the

16 studies involving outcomes, 14, or 88%, showed positive results (Folsom et al., 2005, p. 22).

Career courses can be designed to address a broad range of learning outcomes. Brown and Crane (as cited in Folsom et al., 2005) describe five distinct components included in a comprehensive approach and recommend that a course address no less than three. The five include:

1. Allow clients to clarify career and life goals in writing
2. Provide clients with individualized interpretations and feedback, for example, test results
3. Provide current information on the risks and rewards of selected occupations and career fields
4. Include study of models and mentors who demonstrate effective career behavior
5. Assistance in developing support networks for pursuing career aspirations (p. 7)

There are a variety of learning outcome measures for developing and assessing effective personal career courses, making it hard to synthesize general themes. Despite the variation, a few general dimensions can be identified.

Personal Development. Career maturity and career decidedness are two measurable learning outcomes with a history of research. Career maturity is defined as "an individual's ability to make a realistic career decision," and career decidedness is "a person's level of certainty in their career choices" (Pascarella and Terenzini, 2005, p. 499).

Research conducted by Ganster and Lovell (as cited in Raphael, 2005) utilized the Career Maturity Inventory to assess career development seminar participants. They learned that the participants "viewed work as a more important part of their life than they had prior to the seminar," that their "personal involvement and investment in the career choice process and independence in decision-making increased," and that students were better able to both "identify their own skills and abilities" and "clarify their career goals and solve problems that may arise during the process" (p. 35).

Skills Development. Further examples of successful career courses will be discussed in detail and within the context of specific student populations in Chapter Six. A basic set of skill-specific learning outcomes might include:

- Student demonstrates an ability to differentiate among a variety of industries and roles.
- Student is more aware of graduate school options, admission processes, and acceptance rates.

- Student can identify the relationships among three possible majors and describe related career options for each.
- Student can articulate relevant experiences and successes in a resume.
- Student is very confident in her ability to present herself during the mock interview assignment.
- Student identifies one habit to change upon completion of a personal online reputation audit.

Variation in Design. Career courses are implemented with success across a variety of institutions and with a variety of designed outcomes in mind. Additionally, students and organizations have measured positive results across a wide range of outcomes. This section will illustrate a variety of successful practices across a wide range of campuses. Each of the examples that follow show how a single campus took a variety of inputs and designed a unique curriculum to meet the needs of their students, as well as the organizational and learning outcomes they defined.

When reading and thinking about the reader's own campus, much can be learned from each of the unique cases. Here are some points to consider when researching, developing, or evaluating a career course:

- How have academic culture and values influenced the curriculum?
- How have academic culture and values influenced partners and stakeholders?
- Who was involved in curricular design? in its instruction?
- Which class year was best suited to benefit from the learning goals?
- Was the course for credit? Was it required?
- Was the material integrated into existing academic coursework or taught separately?
- Which combination(s) of curricular methods were effective for their students?
- Which topics needed to be covered to accomplish the outcomes they had defined?
- How was the course assessed and with whom were the results and impact shared?

General Career Courses. Career courses that are general in nature and not major-specific are the most common type of career courses offered in institutions of higher education. While the number of credits associated with the courses may vary, they typically cover the same topics: self-assessment, career choice, and career planning, whether it is planning for graduate school or the world of work. One example of a general career course that prepares students for their next career step is listed below, and additional case studies can be found in Chapter Six.

NEW DIRECTIONS FOR STUDENT SERVICES • DOI: 10.1002/ss

Florida State University's *SDS3340: Introduction to Career Development* is a variable credit course that has existed since 1974 (Vernick, Reardon, and Sampson, Jr., 2002). Taught jointly by career center staff and graduate students, it is a comprehensive curricular approach to career and life planning. It is divided into three components: career concepts and applications, social conditions affecting career development, and implementing a strategic career plan (Florida State University, n.d.). Numerous studies have been conducted on this career course, including an examination of its effects on retention and academic performance.

Major-Specific Career Courses. There are a myriad of ways to approach a program- or major-specific career curriculum. It appears that business programs may participate in career courses more than other academic departments, and these examples have been chosen to illustrate patterns and lessons that can provide inspiration to those across academic disciplines. The following are two curricular approaches to students' transition to life after college via major-specific career courses. The second example in particular provides a modern twist by exploring how the skills and modes of thinking acquired in the classroom can be directly applicable to the process of the job search. It illustrates how a course in social media and marketing provides a platform for students to establish and monitor their own professional brand.

A Multiyear Approach. A collaborative effort between the Career and Academic Planning Center and the College of Business (COB) at Rowan University led to three defined career-relevant learning outcomes and seven corresponding career modules being integrated directly into business courses. The multiyear approach integrated these outcomes:

- Provide freshman COB students with systematic self-assessment, as well as career and business major exploration
- Provide junior-year COB students with the skills necessary for a successful job search
- Teach senior-year COB students how to prepare for interviews (Damminger, Pritchard, Potter, McCalla-Wriggins, 2007)

Social Media as a Learning Opportunity. Champlain College offers *MKT 25: Internet-Based Marketing*, which provides an in-depth examination of Internet marketing, including current innovations, ethical issues, and tactics. A semester-long, group-based project solving an Internet marketing challenge for real-world businesses helps students apply their learning. "Heavy use of the Internet, website analysis, consumer behavior, and integrated media, along with knowledge of current events and changes in e-marketing" are required (Champlain College, 2010). Students are taught to utilize various forms of social media, which are frequently used by both job seekers and employers and are part of the self-marketing and branding strategies taught by career centers (Champlain College, 2010).

New Directions for Student Services • DOI: 10.1002/ss

Transition to Work. It appears that career courses address the transition to work more often than the transition to further education. This section explores four different types of curricular interventions that support a student's transition from a four-year college into the world of work. They are:

- Institutional umbrella programs that include many goals and supports, of which career development is one
- Programs that have been designed to meet career needs unique to a specific population
- Approaches that integrate a specific academic curriculum with career development
- Integration of curriculum and career development, with a focus on using classroom learning to enhance the process of professional development and job searching

As student affairs practitioners learn more through their own and others' research about the diverse students they serve and how needs of different populations can vary dramatically, creating a career curriculum that is specific to certain student populations could be an idea for future development of career courses. Given that programming tailored for specific student populations has proven to be popular and well received, therein lies the opportunity to design a career course focused on diversity.

Graduate and Professional Programs to Work. Career education for graduate students transitioning from their coursework into the professional world can include both transferable and specialized skills. Some students have very defined professional goals that are intertwined with their academic curriculum; others, especially those who are transitioning from research-driven degrees towards professional pursuits outside of academia, may be making dramatic shifts. Examples of career coursework within the graduate student realm are not widespread, but are more easily found within professional schools than academic programs. As the realities of the academic job market continue to become more challenging, this could be seen as an opportune time to include new information and approaches.

Addressing Professional Skills. In response to shifts within the profession and rising expectations with the American Physical Therapy Association (APTA), faculty at Northeastern University developed and assessed a curricular model that explicitly includes students' professional skills (Hayword and Blackmer, 2007). The APTA described seven core values for the Doctorate in Physical Therapy (accountability, altruism, compassion and caring, excellence, integrity, professional duty, and social responsibility) that provide guidance toward designing student learning outcomes (as cited in Hayword and Blackmer, 2007).

With input from a variety of sources, an instructional team created rubrics representing both necessary and damaging job, learning, and professional skills. A multipronged learning process was built around groups of three to five students working toward a shared clinical goal. Students prepared an interaction with a simulated patient through a process that included discussing the case with peers in an online forum. The actual thirty-minute interaction with the simulated patient is videotaped for review by the student and others. The rubrics are then used for the student, simulated patient, peers, and faculty to provide feedback (Hayword and Blackmer, 2007). Since incorporating this curricular approach, students have reported a number of improvements including increased confidence, reduced anxiety, improved ability to integrate and apply academic material with a patient, and an appreciation for the importance of planning and prioritization (Hayword and Blackmer, 2007).

Online Career Course and Services. The Career Services office at Golden Gate University took a very different approach to career curriculum with their population of 4,000 graduate and 700 undergraduate students. Golden Gate University's students are primarily working adults seeking business, tax, and accounting-related degrees, with many of them international students. In addition, Golden Gate has no residential population, and many students take coursework online (NACE, 2010a).

Their career course, required for all undergraduate students, and career services reflect the needs of their students, many of whom desire job acquisition and career management tools more than career exploration assistance. Emphasis is placed upon the virtual career center, including continuous access to self-directed career management tools. Consistent with this shift, staff have specifically trained in distance counseling, and a focus on virtual resources also includes a career newsletter, LinkedIn group, and Twitter feed (NACE, 2010a).

Transition to Graduate Education. There are countless differences between undergraduate and graduate education. Whether it is the graduate admissions processes (for example, providing a writing sample, creating a resume, participating in an interview process) or the actual requirements of the graduate or professional program, they can make students' transition to graduate or professional education challenging. However, some colleges have developed courses that assist students in preparing for graduate and professional school.

St. John Fisher College. When the career center was requested to assist with finding interview partners with field-specific experience, a faculty-led, one-credit, required skills development course for biology majors in their junior year became a collaborative endeavor (Valentino and Freeman, 2010). Students in the biology department at St. John Fisher College typically have career paths that require further education. Thus, a course was designed to educate students about and facilitate the transitional process. Topics included in the curriculum were making career choices, researching graduate programs, understanding the application process, financing additional education, appropriate entrance exams, interviewing, resumes, portfolio, and professional etiquette (Valentino and Freeman, 2010, p. 30).

The mock interview was presented in the first year as a one-night program called Mock Interview Night and featured one interviewer (Professor Edward A. Freeman). In hindsight, this was considered to be less effective than an alternate format with a number of active professionals with expertise across a variety of fields. Professor Freeman reached out to the career center for support in identifying and securing professionals as interviewers and preparing students for a redesigned capstone event. Three goals were established for Mock Interview Night:

1. Provide students with feedback on their level of preparation for graduate and professional programs
2. Provide students with a valuable and realistic interview experience
3. Introduce students to local professionals who might serve as ongoing mentors to the students (Valentino and Freeman, 2010, p. 30)

In addition to these impacts, additional benefits were realized across the university. First, the career center, formerly underutilized by students in scientific pursuits, has seen notable increases in student participation (Valentino and Freeman, 2010). Second, stronger alumni and professional ties in the medical and scientific professions have been realized as a result of the outreach and positive interactions. Initial outreach to St. John Fisher alumni has snowballed and now also includes community members, faculty colleagues, and referrals from current and past participants. Third, several departments across the college are now creating collaborative courses based upon this successful model (Valentino and Freeman, 2010).

University of Texas (UT). The credo of the Intellectual Entrepreneurship Consortium at the University of Texas is *educating citizen-scholars.* Consistent with that credo, UT created a combined credit-bearing course and internship experience to:

> connect undergraduates with faculty and veteran graduate students in their field of study to explore those unique aspects of graduate study that make it distinct from the undergraduate experience (for example, conducting research, writing for scholarly audiences, participating in seminars, serving as teaching and research assistants, publishing articles in professional journals, becoming members of scholarly organizations and learned societies, preparing for an academic or professional career, etc.). (University of Texas, n.d.a)

Any UT undergraduate student who meets minimal criteria and has arranged a supervised project or research with a graduate student or faculty member can apply for participation in the program. Project accountability is determined by the mentoring supervisor, while course activities and assignments are given with the oversight of a graduate student instructor.

Course participation includes four monthly meetings throughout the semester, interactive assignments and presentations, contributions to online discussion boards, and a final essay. Students interview faculty and graduate students to gain insight into how the person has made personal and professional choices, their past experiences and career trajectory, expectations and culture, and how they set and achieved goals throughout their career. Final essays are reflective exercises challenging students to engage with their own learning over the course of the semester (University of Texas, n.d.b).

Capstone Courses

Another example of a curricular approach is capstone courses. Capstone courses are offered almost exclusively at the end of a student's academic program and can be used to measure a student's achievement, as well as the effectiveness of the academic program itself. Students may complete a final project, presentation, or portfolio to demonstrate achievement of student learning and/or program outcomes. These requirements may be related to the student's transition to life after college, whether it be to further education or to work, and such courses may involve mentors, college professors, employers, or a combination of these.

Internships for Credit

A final curricular approach that addresses the transition to after-college life is internships for credit. These courses can vary in credit, and students may engage in these internships at any time during their sophomore to senior years in an undergraduate program, as well as in a graduate or professional program. These courses usually involve a representative from the college (usually an advisor, professor, or career services staff member) and a representative from the company or organization at which the student is interning (usually the supervisor or an internship coordinator). Part of the application process for the internship associated with the for-credit class may involve creating a resume or cover letter, in addition to an interview. Furthermore, business etiquette and professional networking opportunities may be built into the internship itself. All of these components address the preparation for and the transition into life after college, particularly into the world of work.

Conclusion

There are several types of curricular approaches to addressing the transition to life after college. Whether it is an articulation agreement, a career course taught by a career services professional, a major-specific course taught by faculty, a capstone course, or an internship for credit, they all share a common goal: to facilitate students' transition to further education or work as smoothly as possible. The purpose of this chapter is to serve as an overview of the curricular approaches to the transition to after-college life. The next chapter focuses on specific case studies of curricular approaches.

References

20 U.S.C. § Chapter 28, Subchapter IV, Part F, 2010.

Bakersfield College. "Tech Prep California: The Kern/South Tulare Consortium." Retrieved Aug. 12, 2011, from http://www2.bc.cc.ca.us/techprep/articulation.html, 2006.

Champlain College. "Internet-Based Marketing: MKT 250." Retrieved Aug. 12, 2011, from http://classlist.champlain.edu/show/course/number/MKT_250, 2010.

Damminger, J. K., Pritchard, R. E., Potter, G. C., and McCalla-Wriggins, B. "A Collaborative, Holistic Career Development Program for Business Students." *NACE Journal*, March 2007.

Florida State University. "SDS 3340: Introduction to Career Development." Retrieved Aug. 12, 2001, from http://www.career.fsu.edu/courses/sds3340, n.d.

Folsom, B., Reardon, R., and Lee, D. "The Effects of College Career Courses on Learner Outputs and Outcomes" (No. 44). Tallahassee, FL: Florida State University. Retrieved Dec. 5, 2010, from http://www.career.fsu.edu/documents/technical%20reports/technical%20report%2044.doc, 2005.

Hayward, L., and Blackmer, B. "A 360-Degree Assessment Model for Integrating Technical and Professional Skills to Facilitate Successful Workplace Transition." Retrieved Dec. 8, 2010, from http://www.naceweb.org/foundation/done/360degree/, 2007.

Indiana Commission for Higher Education. "Core Transfer Library." Retrieved Aug. 12, 2001, from http://www.transferin.net/CTL.aspx, n.d.

Kansas State Department of Education. "Creating an Articulation Agreement." Retrieved July 29, 2011, from http://www.ksde.org, n.d.

National Association of Colleges and Employers. "2009 Career Services Benchmark Survey for Two-Year Colleges." Bethlehem, PA, 2009.

National Association of Colleges and Employers. "Best Practices: Teaching the Importance of Online Personal Brands." NACE Spotlight Online for Career Services Professionals. Retrieved Dec. 2, 2010, from http://www.naceweb.org/Publications/Spotlight_Online/2010/0331/Best_Practices__Teaching_the_Importance_of_Online_Personal_Brands.aspx?referal=knowledgecenter&menuid=0, 2010a.

National Association of Colleges and Employers. "NACE 2009–2010 Career Services Benchmark Survey for Four-Year Colleges and Universities." Bethlehem, PA, 2010b.

Pascarella, E. T., and Terenzini, P. T. *How College Affects Students* (2nd ed.). San Francisco: Jossey-Bass, 2005.

Raphael, A. "Career Courses: How We Know What Students Are Learning." *NACE Journal*, Fall 2005.

University of North Carolina. "Comprehensive Articulation Agreement." Retrieved Aug. 12, 2011, from http://www.northcarolina.edu/aa/articulation/index.htm, n.d.

University of Texas. "IE Pre-Graduate School Internship." Retrieved Dec. 10, 2010, from University of Texas, Austin, Intellectual Entrepreneurship Consortium Website, communication.utexas.edu/ie, n.d.a.

University of Texas. "Pre-Graduate School Internship Syllabus." Retrieved Dec. 10, 2010, from University of Texas, Austin, Intellectual Entrepreneurship Consortium Website, communication.utexas.edu/ie/syllabus, n.d.b.

Valentino, L., and Freeman, E. "Career Center, Faculty, Alumni Build Mock Interview Program Together: A Collaboration between Career Center and Faculty Yields Benefits for All." *NACE Journal*, April 2010.

Vernick, S. H., Reardon, R. C., and Sampson, Jr., J. P. "Process and Evaluation of a Career Course: A Replication and Extension (Technical Report 31)." Tallahassee, FL: Florida State University. Retrieved Aug. 12, 2011, from http://career.fsu.edu /documents/technical%20reports/Technical%20Report%2031/Technical%20 Report%2031.htm, 2002.

Virginia Tidewater Consortium for Higher Education. Retrieved Aug. 6, 2011, from http://www.vtc.odu.edu, 2008.

CAMEO V. HARTZ is a senior assistant director of the Career Center at Duke University.

JILL PARKER is the director of Advising, Career, and Retention Services at Front Range Community College–Larimer Campus.

NEW DIRECTIONS FOR STUDENT SERVICES • DOI: 10.1002/ss

6

This chapter provides an overview of the career courses adapted by three universities to support the career transition process for each of their student populations. Each university varies by size, location, student population, and approach in the support of the career development needs of their students.

Case Studies of Curricular Approaches

Ann G. Mills and Janice Sutera

As students face the transition to after-college life, whether it be to further education or to the workplace, their choice of classes can determine how well they are prepared. Students obtain a broad knowledge of various subjects through general education classes and more specific knowledge through their particular discipline or major, and often choose electives to augment or enhance the knowledge of their discipline. Additionally, many students add official minors or groups of courses in such areas as languages, writing, technology, business, global affairs, or mathematics based on their interests or as a result of job market trends. These courses may, or may not, intentionally and purposefully focus on helping students make the transition to life after college.

Numerous institutions of higher education provide after-college transition programs through capstone, synthesis, or internship courses. It is less common for an institution to advocate for an ongoing, targeted course curriculum that prepares students to enter the workplace, despite consistent and repeated messages from employers indicating that students entering the workplace lack communication skills, flexibility, tactfulness, initiative, and teamwork skills (National Association of Colleges and Employers [NACE], 2010). The findings from NACE's annual survey of employers regarding their expectations of college graduates are clear: The primary skill set that employers consistently seek and that students consistently lack is communication skills (NACE, 2010, 2009, 2008).

The previous chapter discusses a variety of ways in which curriculum can be used to address the transition to after-college life. In this chapter, the authors discuss college to workplace or graduate school transition courses at three universities: George Mason University, Louisiana State University,

New Directions for Student Services, no. 138, Summer 2012 © Wiley Periodicals, Inc.
Published online in Wiley Online Library (wileyonlinelibrary.com) • DOI: 10.1002/ss.20007

and University of North Carolina–Charlotte. Course designs, target student populations, academic credit, and campus support vary, but all of the courses aim to enhance student skills including self-knowledge, communication, research, and job-search skills in preparation for student transition to employment or graduate/professional school.

George Mason University

With NACE national employer data as a catalyst, University Career Services at George Mason University (hereafter known as Mason) conducted a survey of employers who recruit on campus. The survey sought to identify the skill gaps of Mason students from the employers' perspectives. Specifically, employers stated that students needed to improve their:

- Understanding of who they are and how "who they are" translates to the world of work
- Research of employers to identify how they can impact the work/mission of an organization
- Ability to market themselves to an employer
- Discernment of their market value in today's economy

University Career Services at Mason addressed the issue in a number of ways, one of which was to redesign UNIV 400, a one-credit transition course for second-semester juniors and seniors offered in two differently focused curricula. One curriculum devotes attention to the college-to-workplace transition, and three or more sections of this version are offered each semester. The other version applies its focus to the college-to-graduate school transition, and one section is offered each semester. Both versions emphasize student self-assessment, job search skills, resume development, interview practice, and setting career goals.

Advertisement of the classes to students begins during preregistration in the semester before enrollment. More intense marketing to faculty advisors and students occurs just before the semester begins and ends after the first week of the course add period. A minimum of four class sections, with an enrollment of up to twenty students per section, are offered in both fall and spring semesters. College to Workplace sections are typically taught by employers who have recruited or interacted extensively with college students and/or by experienced career counselors. The College to Graduate School section is typically taught by a university staff member who is familiar with student development and a wide variety of higher education resources for students who are seriously considering graduate school. Qualified state employees may receive compensation for teaching beyond their regular working hours. Employers and others serving as instructors are paid as adjunct faculty. The one-credit course meets weekly for 110 minutes.

NEW DIRECTIONS FOR STUDENT SERVICES • DOI: 10.1002/ss

A program manager in University Career Services recruits and hires the instructors, develops and revises the curriculum, and manages the assessment of outcomes report for the courses. Until 2006, UNIV 400 was wholly managed by staff in the office of Student Academic Affairs, Advising, and Retention. University Career Services assumed management responsibility when it was determined that University Career Services' substantive college-to-career expertise would benefit students. Consequently, a documented partnership between the two offices was formed. The UNIV 400 courses are part of a series of career transition course offerings that include the following: UNIV 200–Major/Career Decisions (2 credits) and UNIV 300–Confirming Majors/Careers: Pursuing Internships (1 credit). The courses are a key part of the portfolio of student career development programs managed by University Career Services in collaboration with Student Academic Affairs, Advising and Retention.

College to Workplace. The workplace sections enhance the students' ability to market and present themselves to employers, as well as to develop the students' understanding of their chosen fields through informational interviewing. This section will describe the learning objectives, assignments, rubrics, and student feedback for this version of the course.

Learning Objectives. Each section of the workplace version of UNIV 400 assesses five core learning objectives using corresponding rubrics for each objective. The learning objectives for the College to Workplace sections are as follows:

1. Students will be able to write a targeted resume and cover letter for an employer who matches their interests, skills, and qualifications.
2. Students will be able to deliver a clear 30- to 60-second targeted marketing pitch to an employer that connects the student's background with the mission of the organization.
3. Students will be able to provide specific examples to questions they receive in a behavioral mock interview using the Situation-Task-Action-Results (STAR) model.
4. Students will identify an alumnus or employer in their field of interest, conduct an informational interview, and produce a two-page report.
5. Students will develop a career plan that integrates their self-knowledge with their career choice, including a career plan B and a plan C.

Assignments. Originally the UNIV 400 program required students to write papers demonstrating their comprehension of course objectives. As a result of the 2008 employer survey feedback, the program manager redesigned the course so students could more actively engage in classroom discussion with their classmates and the instructor. In both the workplace and

New Directions for Student Services • DOI: 10.1002/ss

the graduate school course curricula, instructors found class participation critical to student success. Therefore, in-class participation represents 25 percent of a student's grade. In addition, students schedule a one-on-one meeting with the instructor during the semester to discuss their specific career concerns, goals, or transition issues, and this meeting also counts toward the participation portion of the grade.

Other graded course assignments include: a targeted resume, a job fair presentation with marketing pitch to an employer attending the fair (oral), a practice interview (oral), an informational interview with a professional in the student's field of interest, and a career plan. Each assignment represents 15 percent of the student's grade. Well-defined rubrics aid instructors and students in understanding course assignments and expectations.

Rubrics. The program manager for UNIV 400 developed a set of rubrics for each of the five assignments in the course. The rubrics define criteria and standards used to assess a student's performance on papers, projects, essays, and other assignments. Rubrics translate the quality of the student work in light of the learning objectives and the intended outcomes of the course. Using the rubrics to assess student learning outcomes help the program manager and instructors identify curriculum changes needed to effect student behavioral change, enhance critical thinking, and impact student development.

The rubrics for each of the five learning objectives in the College to Workplace course promote student understanding of assignments and encourage successful completion. Instructors provide the students with the rubrics when giving the assignments in class and identify examples of quality work. Rubrics for each assignment divide performance factors into three levels or categories: *developing, competent,* and *exemplary.* Using class time, each instructor answers student questions about the criteria for developing competent and exemplary performance on the assignment. The rubric performance categories clarify expectations of students at each level and inform the grading policies of each instructor. The rubrics also encourage consistency in assignment expectations across all sections of the College to Workplace course.

The following rubric (Table 6.1) is an example of one used in the College to Workplace class that addresses the student's skill in developing the personal pitch he/she will use with an employer. Each of the three separate rubric blocks is labeled with the name of the skill/competency that the instructor is seeking to teach the student.

In this personal pitch rubric the student is provided with the criteria defining exemplary performance for the assignment. Instructors use the rubric criteria to guide their work as they prepare the students to present themselves to employers at the job and internship fair. Two weeks prior to the fair, students research three or more employers of interest and develop statements that identify who they are and how their backgrounds relate to the work of the employer. Instructors coach students during UNIV 400

Table 6.1 George Mason University's College to Workplace Transition 30- to 60-Second Pitch Rubric (7 items)

Student Name:

Employer Research

Student identifies at least 3 employers who hire in their field (employer may/may not be attending the job/ internship fair).

Student is comfortable using resources to aid in employer research.

Student Self-Assessment

Student identifies the work values (e.g., hires in my major, good location, good benefits, financially stable, etc.) important to him/her.

Knowing his/her values, interests, and skills, student is able to integrate employer research to identify employers who will be a good fit.

Synthesis; Oral Communication Skills

Student easily identifies who he/she is, the major/school, and the kind of position in which he/she is interested.

Student "hooks" the employer with previous experience statement or information about himself/herself that would be of interest to the employer.

Student asks appropriate follow-up question(s).

Rubric Scoring: Instructor identifies up to 7 items that define the student's level of competency.

Exemplary (7 items)

Competent (5–6 items)

Developing (fewer than 5 items)

class time on how to use the information gleaned in researching employers and provide students the opportunity to practice introducing themselves. Students practice eye contact, handshakes, and self-marketing pitches in preparation for the fair. These rubrics guide UNIV 400 students in enhancing their preparation and confidence as they rehearse their self-presentation to potential employers.

Student Feedback. Based on data gathered from all the UNIV 400 workplace instructors during the Spring 2011 term, 89 percent of students who enrolled in UNIV 400 completed assignments that were evaluated as "competent" or "exemplary" under the framework of all five rubrics.

Of course, hearing from the students in the class provides useful insights as well. Three students who completed the UNIV 400 workplace transition course in 2011 commented:

NEW DIRECTIONS FOR STUDENT SERVICES • DOI: 10.1002/ss

… this class has by far been the most useful class I have taken in my college career. I give full credit to this class for the internship I was able to receive as well as the life knowledge I received along the way. You are one of the most beneficial professors that I have ever come in contact with and truly do thank you for all of the knowledge you have provided me with. It is clear that you are a teacher who actually loves to teach.

Thank you so much for your tips, advice, and guidelines throughout the semester. This "College to Workplace" course was really a big help to prepare me for a career and most importantly, my future. Some of the subjects that were discussed in class I had no idea about. The speakers were a big help/influence also.

Their discussion and experiences were interesting to listen to because they were once in our shoes and it was easier to ask questions and for them to relate to us. The assignments and exercises that you had the class do were helpful and prepared me for life after graduation. Thanks so much!

College to Graduate School. The graduate school section prepares students to research and effectively apply to graduate programs, as well as to reflect on their decision-making processes regarding the graduate or professional programs they select. This section will describe the learning objectives, assignments, rubrics, and student feedback for this version of the course.

Learning Objectives. The College to Graduate School section of UNIV 400 assesses five learning objectives using corresponding rubrics for each objective. The course objectives are as follows:

1. Students will be able to write a targeted resume and cover letter for a graduate program that matches their interests, skills, and qualifications.
2. Students will be able to write a personal statement targeted to the graduate program to which they would like to apply.
3. Students will practice their interviewing skills in a mock graduate school interview scenario.
4. Students will identify an alumnus or employer in their field of interest, conduct an informational interview, and produce a two-page report.
5. Students will develop a career plan that integrates their self-knowledge with their career options, including a career plan B and plan C.

Assignments. The graduate school section assignments are the same as those for the workplace section except that students in the graduate school section submit a personal statement written for a graduate program or professional school in place of the job fair presentation. The College to

Graduate School course uses five graded assignments and includes a class participation grade (25 percent). The five assignments include: a targeted resume and cover letter, a personal statement for one graduate program, an informational interview report, a practice interview, and a career plan. The assignments and participation in both classes focus on strengthening the students' written and oral communication skills because employers indicate that students lack such communication skills.

Rubrics. Similar to the College to Workplace class, the rubrics guide the students and the instructors on learning outcomes and assessment of the assignments. The rubric category labels are "developing," "competent," and "exemplary." Students find that the rubrics provide guidance, define expectations on assignments, and create an opportunity for conversation with the instructor. Overall, the rubrics receive positive feedback from instructors and students.

The following rubric (Table 6.2) assesses the informational interview assignment. It is used in both the College to Graduate School and the College to Workplace classes.

The informational interview assignment engages the student in self-reflection regarding how he or she will apply the graduate degree they are exploring in their chosen career field. The goal of the assignment is for the student to consider several questions. Is the graduate degree necessary for my chosen profession? How is the profession I am considering a reflection of my interests, values, and skills? What experience is required to enter this profession and what career-related experience do I have or might I want to obtain before I enter this field? Students who successfully complete this assignment are able to answer the questions, identify at least one contact in the field, and decide if graduate school is an immediate goal or part of the student's future career plans.

Student Feedback. Based on data gathered by the instructors, 93 percent of students enrolled in the UNIV 400 Graduate School section during the Spring 2011 term completed assignments that were evaluated as "competent" or "exemplary" under the framework of all five rubrics.

Student comments from the College to Graduate School course include:

> This is the first university course I have taken where someone taught me how to develop a budget—a skill I will be able to use for a lifetime! I'm not sure I'm ready to assume graduate school loans yet.

> This course forced me to research whether or not a graduate degree was really necessary for me to achieve my short-term career goals. I think I'll be putting off graduate school for two or three years.

> This course helped me write an improved personal statement for graduate school. It also helped me prepare for an interview and also improve my job-hunting skills since I'll need to work while in graduate school.

NEW DIRECTIONS FOR STUDENT SERVICES • DOI: 10.1002/ss

Table 6.2 George Mason University's College to Workplace Transition Informational Interview Rubric (11 items)

Student Name:

Employer/Career Field Research

Student identifies at least 3 employers and/or alumni who hire in their field or industry.

Student is comfortable using resources to aid in employer/alumni research.

Research and Communication Skills

Student asks questions designed to learn about the contact's educational background;

Contact's occupation/field;

Issues/trends in contact's field;

And how best to prepare for this kind of work.

Based on the information the student elicits from the contact during the interview, the student obtains information that aids his/her career decision-making.

Synthesis and Written Communication Skills

Student succinctly develops a well-written report (organized, free of spelling and grammar errors) that

Describes the contact's career field and/or industry,

Defines important points/learning for the student, and

Summarizes how the student will use the results in his/her decision making.

Rubric Scoring: Instructor identifies up to 11 items that define the student's level of competency.

Exemplary (10–11 items)

Competent (8–9 items)

Developing (fewer than 8 items)

The UNIV 400 course continues to change and grow as the student population changes. During the 2009–2010 academic year, approximately 50 percent of the students who enrolled in the course were humanities and social science majors. To meet the specific needs of these students who are challenged to articulate how their skills and knowledge in the liberal arts translate to the world of work, the curriculum has undergone some recent enhancements to include offering two specific sections of the course for humanities and social science students. As part of these sections, the curriculum modules include relevant targeted activities that may be used by all

NEW DIRECTIONS FOR STUDENT SERVICES • DOI: 10.1002/ss

instructors for their students as appropriate. In addition, as part of a grant funded project, a combined version of UNIV 300 (internship-focused) and UNIV 400 for veteran/military students was offered in Fall 2010.

Louisiana State's Strategic Career Development Course

Career Development (HRE 3331) is a three-credit elective offered at Louisiana State University (LSU). The Strategic Career Development course offers a comprehensive approach to career development and career decision making. The class incorporates self-awareness, career exploration, and intensive self-marketing techniques and activities. The curriculum emphasizes networking skills and concentrates on linking personal competencies to organizational needs. Students apply their job search success skills to full-time and internship opportunities.

Learning Objectives. Several learning objectives have been identified for the Strategic Career Development/Planning course. They include:

1. Students will be able to apply career development theory to their career planning process. Specifically, students will: (a) take career assessments and apply their interests, abilities, values, and personality assessments in making career decisions; (b) gather occupational information through resources and info interviewing; and (c) be able to identify career barriers and methods for overcoming them.
2. Students will be able to link personal career competencies to corporate competencies.
3. Students will be able to develop a strategic career plan including a personal marketing plan.
4. Students will understand ethics in the job-search process and in the workplace.
5. Students will be able to demonstrate an understanding of the elements involved in conducting an effective job search including networking, using resources, and interviewing.
6. Students will be able to understand the process of applying to graduate and professional school.

Assignments. The class meets twice per week for 90-minute class periods. To confirm the terms of the class, students sign a contract with the instructor, which is modeled after a job offer contract. Class attendance, discussion, and preparation are critical and expected. Assignments are worth from 15 to 20 percent of the grade. The self-assessment portion of the class uses the TypeFocus™ Careers Program and a values/skills assessment. The self-assessment is not graded.

The Job Search Skills Packet, worth 20 percent of the grade, includes: the final draft of a resume and a copy of the original critiqued resume, final

Table 6.3 Louisiana State University Strategic Career Development Thank-You Note Rubric

	Exemplary	Competent	Developing
Thank-you letter	Written in business format. Free of all spelling and grammar mistakes. Letter demonstrates continued interest, thanks employer for their time, and includes a conclusion statement. Typed on resume paper.	Contains a few spelling and grammar mistakes. Letter is not addressed to a specific person. Date the letter is sent was not included. Not submitted on resume paper.	Contains lots of spelling and grammar mistakes. Letter fails to demonstrate your interest in the company or to thank the employer for their time.

draft of a cover letter and a copy of the original critiqued cover letter, research worksheet on an organization, two-minute commercial, and thank-you letter (see the rubric sample in Table 6.3); and interview feedback sheets from in-class practice interview and employer mock interview. The student's informational interview, personal statement, and job-shadowing assignments are each worth 15 percent of the grade. The job-shadowing assignment requires the student to observe a professional for four hours on a typical workday. Students also take a mid-term exam worth 15 percent of the grade. Finally, a reflection paper and presentation worth 20 percent of the student's grade requires the student to respond to several questions. Who am I? Where am I going? Where might I anticipate areas of struggle and what will help me overcome these issues? What are my timelines? What might stand in the way of my timelines and how might I overcome those factors? What are my three most important life goals and how might they be impacted by my career choice? What do I still want to know?

Beyond the graded assignments, special features of the course include an in-class fashion show demonstrating professional dress, a mid-course recruiter panel offering a real world view from the employer perspective, and a mock job search culminating in a practice interview with a full-time recruiter. The course also covers preparing for graduate school decisions including researching graduate school options, writing a personal statement, and gleaning advice from a graduate student panel. Instructors encourage students who need supplemental instruction and individualized career development assistance to arrange for individual appointments with the instructor or with other career service professionals in the Career Services office.

Rubrics. All evaluative rubrics are available to the students at the beginning of the semester with corresponding instructions for each assignment. Instructors use the rubrics as a guide for grading, and students may reference the rubrics as they work on assignments and projects (see Table 6.3).

Student Comments. This course gives students the opportunity to improve their skill levels and sense of self-direction as they explore fields of interest and evaluate how their skills and values might fit into those fields. Ideally, students experience increased confidence in their ability to successfully navigate the job search and to secure appropriate and satisfying employment. Positive course evaluations and open student feedback illustrate the impact of the course. Student comments at the end of the semester have included the following:

> Great course. I strongly feel that my new position with the U.S. Department of Labor was in part due to the instruction provided in this course.

> This course was great. I think it should be mandatory for students. It provided me with the skills to find a job, apply for it, interview, and get it!

> This course should be required for sophomores and juniors. This excellent course taught me so much about searching for a career and surviving the real world. The more you put into this course, the more you get out of it.

Course Management. Created in collaboration with the Human Resource Education Department and offered through the School of Human Resources Education and Workforce Development, LSU Career Services staff is wholly responsible for curriculum design and instruction. Students must have sophomore standing or higher or gain instructor permission to enroll. LSU offers one section of the course each fall and spring semester. Course enrollment is limited to 30 students. Typically, two Career Services staff members share instructional duties for different portions of the curriculum based on their Career Services job specializations. A graduate assistant (GA) supports the two instructors. The GA provides administrative assistance and receives professional development and academic credit in their higher education program of study.

This course features career development theory, includes decision-making for graduate study, and provides more extensive curriculum activities and assignments than the one-credit offerings at Mason.

UNC-Charlotte: College Transition Transfers

College Transition Transfers (UCOLL 1011) is a three-credit transfer seminar course offered at the University of North Carolina-Charlotte

(UNC-Charlotte). One of the three or four sections taught each semester specifically focuses on career issues.

Learning Objectives. The five learning objectives of the College Transition Transfers career seminar are as follows.

1. Learn about the University and become familiar with resources available on campus
2. Build supportive relationships during the transition from a previous college/university to UNC-Charlotte
3. Become familiar with the career development cycle and University Career Center (UCC) resources, including the Career Resource Library, workshops and special events, career advising, and experiential learning opportunities such as job shadowing, internships, and cooperative education
4. Develop skills for academic, personal, and career success at UNC-Charlotte and beyond
5. Strengthen oral communication skills, thus fulfilling the University's oral communication requirement

Assignments. Course assignments include four oral presentations, eight written assignments, several resource worksheets, two career assessments, a resume, a cover letter, and a portfolio, as well as midterm and final exams. The oral presentations include: a three- to five-minute creative presentation to help the class learn more about each student using ideas based on the StoryCorps Project (Isay, 2007), a five- to seven-minute campus involvement presentation on how their participation in a campus group is shaping or will shape their transfer experience, a mock interview presentation where they respond to three interview questions in front of a group, and a twelve- to fifteen-minute presentation on a career field of interest. The evaluation of oral presentations is based 50 percent on content and 50 percent on delivery.

Students complete eight written assignments during the College Transition Transfers course. There are five reflection papers, which are worth 25 points each. The first reflection assignment is a transferring reflection, a written report on why they transferred to UNC Charlotte. The second is a career assessment reflection concentrating on what they learned from the Strong Interest Inventory and Myers-Briggs Type Indicator, and how this information helps them plan for academic and career success.

The third reflection paper of a one-page Career Advisor appointment focuses on what they discussed in the advising appointment about self-assessment and job search topics, as well as how this information will be helpful. The fourth assignment is an event reflection. After attending a career-related event, the student writes a one-page reflection paper addressing what they learned and how this information will help them in their major or career search. If the student attends more than one event, this assignment may be completed more than once for extra credit.

The Internship Reflection paper requires that students find two internship position descriptions in the UNC-Charlotte job/internship database, and address why these opportunities are of interest to them. Also, students must develop two questions for a panel of student interns. In the Diversity Reflection assignment, students reflect on how diversity can benefit today's workplace. Students consider how diversity can positively affect their career and personal success. In the paper students must discuss the steps they can take at UNC-Charlotte to increase their multicultural competence.

In addition, there is an optional Information Interview Report, worth 20 points for extra credit requiring that the student interview a professional in a career field of interest and write about what was learned from that individual. The student should address how the interview experience influenced their view of the career and/or the organization that employs the interviewee.

The final two assignments are the Career Report and the Action Plan. Each is worth 25 points. In addition to an oral presentation on a career field of interest, students submit a two- to three-page written summary of the presentation and cite the sources consulted. Their Career Report must address the following information: (1) nature of the work—roles/responsibilities of professionals in this field; (2) working conditions (that is, hours) and work settings (office compared with outdoors, school compared with corporation, and so on); (3) professional qualifications—types of education, licensure, and/or experience required; (4) trends in the field (projected increases or decreases in employment) and typical salary/earnings; and (5) why the career seems a good fit, incorporating what they learned from the self-assessments.

The purpose of the Action Plan assignment is for the students to chart out their plans for the next semester and for the rest of their time at UNC-Charlotte, including post-graduation plans. The action plan paper addresses the following: how the course assisted the students in their planning for the future, how the students planned for their academic success while at UNC-Charlotte, and how the students continue to research future goals (graduate school, full-time employment, and other opportunities).

Similar to the other career courses mentioned in this chapter, attendance and participation are critical to student success in this course. Participation is worth 10 percent of the grade.

Rubrics. Students receive specific information on how oral content and delivery for their assignment will be evaluated. The rubric for the oral presentations is included in the syllabus. Unlike the other two career transition courses covered in this chapter, this course meets the general education requirement for oral communication in this college's curriculum. As a

Table 6.4 UNC Charlotte Transition Transfers Oral Presentation Rubric

Oral presentations will be graded based on the following criteria. For each presentation, each student will receive written comments and suggestions from the instructors. Effort (and improvement, if applicable) will be taken into consideration.

Content (50%)

- Adequately covers topic/required information
- Introduces main idea at opening
- Provides supporting details
- Uses transitions between different points
- Connects with the audience
- Summarizes topic at conclusion
- Offers visual aids (if required)

Delivery (50%)

- Has appropriate eye contact and facial expressions
- Has appropriate movement and gestures
- Limits use of "filler words" ("um," "like," and other colloquial language)
- Has vocal variation (rate, pitch, volume, articulation pauses)
- Utilizes time effectively (does not go over or under time given)
- Consults notes appropriately (if applicable)
- Divides time equally among group members (if a group presentation)

result, there are more assignments for instructors to assess the students' oral communication skill development. Table 6.4 details the specific factors of content and delivery upon which students are evaluated in this oral communication rubric.

Course Management. Two career services professionals teach the career seminar. One of the instructors for the transfer transition career seminar is the Assistant Director for Transfer Career Programs. Course instruction is part of their job responsibilities. Each semester the career course section enrolls up to 22 students. The course meets twice a week for 75 minutes throughout the 15-week semester. In addition to elective credit, the course can be counted toward UNC-Charlotte's oral communication requirement, providing an extra incentive for student participation and class enrollment. All of the transfer seminars must meet the general education requirement for oral communication.

Conclusion

The case studies in this chapter offer three different curricular approaches taken by universities to prepare their students to transition to the world of work and/or graduate school. The universities' programs vary in the following ways: target audience, program objectives, instructor expertise, number of credits, department accountability and collaboration, and the type of rubrics or evaluative criteria used for assessment of learning outcomes. What appears constant is the relative success of these three universities in developing and facilitating the instruction of the career transition courses. The progress in attainment of learning outcomes is impressive, and the positive student comments are encouraging. No doubt the students' increased sense of self-confidence will be helpful to them as they transition to life after college.

Is there room for improvement? Absolutely! Just as the economy and job market are fluid, so too are students and their learning needs. These programs must continue to stay abreast of the latest developments in the job market as well as of the students so that their transition needs continue to be met. For example, Mason recently adapted its College to Career Transition course to veterans returning to school who have unique employment needs, and specially developed resources on the college campus are incorporated into the course.

Whether an institution is large or small, public or private, two-year or four-year, transition courses for college-to-career or to graduate/professional school are appropriate. As these case studies suggest, a school's particular characteristics are not critical to determining a program's success; instead, designing a program knowing the target audience, resources, learning objectives, and collaborators are the keys to successful outcomes. Once a college-to-career transition program is in place, committed student affairs professionals and faculty, as well as motivated students, are the final elements required to achieve the ultimate college-to-career course outcome: a student population, enriched with self-knowledge and career/occupational research, capable of and confident in making initial and ongoing career/life decisions.

References

Isay, D. *Listening Is an Act of Love: A Celebration of American Life from the StoryCorps Project.* New York: Penguin Press, 2007.

National Association of Colleges and Employers. "Job Outlook 2011." *Job Outlook*, Nov. 2010, 1–35. Retrieved Apr. 30, 2011, from http://www.naceweb.org.

National Association of Colleges and Employers. "Job Outlook 2010." *Job Outlook*, Nov. 2009, 1–33. Retrieved Apr. 30, 2011, from http://www.naceweb.org.
National Association of Colleges and Employers. "Job Outlook 2009." *Job Outlook*, Nov. 2008, 1–42. Accessed Apr. 30, 2011, from http://www.naceweb.org.

ANN G. MILLS *is currently the assistant director of Career and Consulting Services at the George Washington University Career Center. She was formerly the program manager of UNIV 400 at George Mason University.*

JANICE SUTERA *is currently the director at George Mason University Career Services.*

NEW DIRECTIONS FOR STUDENT SERVICES • DOI: 10.1002/ss

7

This chapter looks ahead to consider changes in higher education and other social arenas that might offer challenges and opportunities that can inform how student affairs practitioners and faculty colleagues assist students in preparing for after-college life.

Looking Forward: New Challenges and Opportunities

Elizabeth J. Bushnell

Just as the job market and industry change at a rapid pace, so too must preparation for college graduates entering the workforce or further studies. Such changes have an immediate impact on graduates seeking full-time employment after graduation, but also influence the decisions and success of students pursuing the next level of education, whether a four-year degree or graduate school. It is essential for higher education professionals to remain abreast of industry trends, emerging fields, and changing requirements that affect the job market and advanced education opportunities for new graduates. Equally important is a continual review of evolving strategies for success in the job search itself. Common practices in today's career services office, like marketing events via social media and coaching students to polish their online presence, were unheard of even ten years ago.

This chapter explores recent job market trends and emerging industries, reviews changes in the job search process, and evaluates how changes in higher education transform the preparation of graduates. It also looks ahead to consider how changes in the job market and job search process might alter the ways in which practitioners prepare college graduates for their futures. Finally, this chapter addresses how changes in higher education may further influence the approach of student affairs professionals and their colleagues as they prepare new generations of college students for after-college life.

Job Market Changes

The United States (U.S.) Department of Labor's Bureau of Labor Statistics (B.L.S.) develops updated employment projections every two years,

New Directions for Student Services, no. 138, Summer 2012 © Wiley Periodicals, Inc.
Published online in Wiley Online Library (wileyonlinelibrary.com) • DOI: 10.1002/ss.20008

providing useful data for anticipating job market changes through *The Occupational Outlook Quarterly* publication; its most recent edition highlights projections for the decade from 2008 to 2018 (Bureau of Labor Statistics, 2010c). Reviews of current data inform practitioners of occupations with increasing opportunities as well as changes in educational requirements. Current B.L.S. data indicate that professional and related occupations, such as health care, science, education, and information technology; and service occupations, such as protection and consumer services, are expected to gain the most new jobs and produce the greatest number of job openings through 2018 (B.L.S., 2010c). Nearly half of all new jobs and one third of job openings require a postsecondary degree or certificate. Findings support the ongoing shift from a goods-producing to a service-providing economy and increasing demand for an educated workforce. Some job market changes result from growth in existing industries, while others stem from new and emerging fields. A review of current job market trends provides insight into challenges and opportunities for schools in their preparation of college graduates.

Health Care Industry. Already one of the largest industries in 2008, the Bureau of Labor Statistics projects that health care will generate more new jobs than any other industry through 2018 (2010c). Rapid increase in the elderly population accounts for much of this growth. However, actual job creation may advance even more dramatically if health-care reform vastly increases coverage for those currently uninsured, thereby driving up demand for health-care services. Half of the 20 fastest growing jobs are health-care related, including biomedical engineers, physician assistants, and athletic trainers (B.L.S., 2010c). Although most health-care occupations require less than a bachelor's degree, at least half require some postsecondary training (Bureau of Labor Statistics, 2010a). As the largest and fastest-growing industry, health-care careers provide a multitude of opportunities for new graduates. Students considering further education in health-care specialties should review not only their own personal fit for the profession, but also varying job-market demands for specific occupations within the wide-ranging health-care field. For instance, demand for dental assistants is projected to grow by 105,600 jobs by 2018, compared to projected demand for over half a million new registered nurses in the same time range (Bureau of Labor Statistics, n.d.). Current trends in the health-care field, such as automation of health-care records, increasing service for an aging population, and legislative changes affecting health-care coverage, suggest that courses in technology, gerontology, and political science may best complement a core science curriculum for those preparing to enter the industry.

Green Jobs. Green jobs have been highly lauded as an emerging sector poised to provide new jobs and economic growth. There is debate on how expansive such growth may be, as well as debate on what constitutes a green job. A 2009 study by Pew Charitable Trusts categorized the clean energy economy as including clean energy, energy efficiency, environmentally friendly production, conservation and pollution mitigation, and training and support. The Bureau of Labor Statistics (2010b) more broadly defines green jobs as either "jobs in businesses that produce goods or provide services that benefit the environment or conserve natural resources" or "jobs in which workers' duties involve making their establishment's production processes more environmentally friendly or use fewer natural resources." Such a broad definition makes the emerging green industry a source of new opportunities in multiple fields for graduates of any major. Just how many opportunities the industry will create is uncertain. Significant expansion in the green jobs industry may be dependent on instrumental changes in the U.S.'s energy system, such as legislative action making other energy sources more expensive, thereby increasing demand for clean energy (Katel, 2010).

Even without such changes, research from Pew Charitable Trusts (2009) reports that clean energy jobs grew at a faster rate than overall jobs during 1998–2007. The Bureau of Labor Statistics just began collecting data on green jobs in Fiscal Year 2010 and may offer more definitive projections in coming years. In response to market demands as well as sustainability interests of students, more universities are offering green degree programs, which vary from core class requirements about the environment to graduate programs combining traditional fields like business or architecture with green curriculum like environmental studies and sustainable design (Berman, 2009). Although the impact of job creation in the green industry is yet unknown, it may yield tremendous educational and career opportunities for new graduates. Students considering such opportunities should develop a basic understanding of energy production and distribution, environmental impact issues, physical and natural sciences, theories of climate change, federal and state regulations, funding opportunities, and innovative approaches for these complex issues.

Entrepreneurialism. In 2009, entrepreneurial activity was at its highest rate in 14 years, according to the Kauffman Index of Entrepreneurial Activity (Kauffman Foundation, 2010). Perhaps driven by the recession and scarcity of traditional jobs, many college graduates seek to create their own opportunities through new businesses. Although the highest rate of business startups is among 35- to 44-year-olds, more young college graduates are pursuing this career path (Madden, 2010). This is a trend likely to continue for college graduates beyond the recession since common characteristics of Millennials—individuals born between the late 1970s and the early 2000s—make them well suited for entrepreneurial pursuits (Howe and Strauss, 2007). Optimism and confidence combined with the technical savvy of the Internet and social media give younger generations the motivation and tools to pursue innovative ideas (Cohen, 2010). Cross-disciplinary training will be essential to budding entrepreneurs. To support students on this path, career services can shift from training on writing resumes and finding jobs to training on writing business plans, finding investors, and networking for clients.

Implications for Practitioners. Remaining abreast of new industries and career opportunities enables practitioners to introduce students to new and expanding fields as well as advise them on the classes, graduate studies, and experiences that can best prepare them. Keeping pace with the changes in industry and professional opportunities presents challenges. No practitioner can be fully versed in every possible career path. However, it's important to introduce students to the possibilities, especially new careers and unlikely connections of majors to emerging industries. Pursuing green jobs is an obvious choice for an environmental studies major, but less so for a business student who might become an energy broker or an art graduate who might become a green interior designer.

Because degree offerings and classes often change at a slower pace than industry, it is especially helpful to teach students which combinations of classes and experiences will enable them to develop competencies for success in new fields and which graduate programs best prepare them for expanding industries. Specific practices may include panel presentations of professionals in emerging industries, networking events for students and alumni in such fields, and career classes that incorporate job market analysis. It is helpful to teach graduates how to recognize industry trends, remain abreast of new practices, and position themselves to take advantage of opportunities as they arise. Although career choice and direction is never based on job market projections alone, such information can inform graduates as they consider and navigate multiple jobs and career paths over their professional lives.

The Evolving Job Search Process

In addition to changes in the job market and occupations themselves, the process for finding jobs is steadily progressing. The most obvious and significant changes are occurring due to advances in technology. Social media and new communication venues are transforming the recruiting and job search process. Resume PDF files uploaded to company websites have replaced mailed applications on crisp resume paper. E-mail blasts and forwarded messages among online networks are replacing job vacancy announcements in the local newspaper. Many tenets of the job search remain: candidates must still network to build connections, stand out among crowded applicant pools, and demonstrate their value to employers, but the processes and steps to do so are evolving. Perhaps the most significant effects of technology are increasing volumes of information, greater access among candidates and employers, and new venues for applying. Employers engage more candidates via virtual recruiting and candidates are able to access more openings. Both encounter greater information about each other via the Internet. Advances in networking opportunities provide

NEW DIRECTIONS FOR STUDENT SERVICES • DOI: 10.1002/ss

new avenues for job seekers to connect and engage with professionals in their fields. All of these changes carry implications for the work of colleges and universities in preparing graduates for life after college.

Impact of Technology. Communication between job seekers and employers is progressing at a swift pace as new technology influences the job search process. In 2009, the National Association of Colleges and Employers (NACE) *Future Trends Survey* (2009) identified technology as one of the most important trends affecting college recruiting, according to both employers and career services professionals. Specifically, respondents indicated that new communication venues and social networking are likely to have the biggest impact.

New Communication Venues. Certainly, current students and young professionals are more accustomed to online communication than previous generations and expect online contact with potential employers. The Internet provides instant access to job listings and company information, and e-mail is a more direct and immediate connection between employers and candidates. New communication venues make virtual recruiting easier and less expensive than traditional means. Company branding, job announcements, applications, job fairs, and even interviews are all available through online forums. Both career services practitioners and employers expect on-campus recruiting to diminish with the increase in online and virtual recruiting (NACE, 2009). For employers, virtual recruiting enables them to reach a broader audience of candidates and schools than they could with on-campus visits. With less on-campus recruiting, the role of career centers as intermediaries to establish connections between candidates and employers will likely change. However, there remains significant need for guidance from colleges and universities to help students navigate voluminous amounts of information online, pursue appropriate e-mail correspondence and application strategies with employers, and get noticed within the wider applicant pool that employers generate through virtual recruiting. Professional and effective use of online communication venues continues to be redefined as new tools emerge and gain prominence in the job search process.

Social Networking. Unsurprisingly, students who have grown up with the Internet and social media are relatively savvy in the use of social networks for personal purposes. Initial efforts by practitioners related to social networking revolved around privacy issues and teaching students to protect personal, potentially negative, information that was now accessible to the public and employers online. In 2010, Cross-Tab found that 79 percent of United States hiring managers research candidates online, and 70 percent report rejecting candidates based on information they found. Online profiles may influence college admissions as well. A Kaplan Test Prep and Admissions Survey in 2010 found that 82 percent of admissions officers use Facebook and other social media in recruiting (*BusinessWire*, 2010).

More students are responding to such realities and are taking steps to protect their online identities. A 2010 report from Pew Research Center showed that young adults, ages 18–29, are the most active in managing their online presence; they are more likely than older users to restrict what they share online and with whom they share it (Pew Internet and American Life Project, 2010). However, beyond protecting their online image, students have much to learn in order to leverage their online presence to their advantage and utilize social networking to advance their job and graduate school prospects. Not only are employers researching candidates online, they are actively using online social networks to recruit new candidates. The 2010 Jobvite Social Recruiting Survey found that employers are spending less on job boards and more on social recruiting, reporting that 83 percent of employers will recruit in social networks this year. Just as negative online information can adversely affect job search success, positive online reputations make a difference to hiring managers. Of recruiters surveyed by Cross-Tab (2010), 85 percent reported that a positive online image influenced their hiring decisions to some extent. There are legal considerations related to the use of personal information available online in the hiring process. Most significantly, recruiters with access to pictures and videos of candidates early in the recruiting process may open the door for allegations of discrimination. However, until there is legal precedence regarding what may or may not be used in recruiting and hiring, the use of social media is a rapidly growing practice among employers. If college graduates are not actively developing and promoting their professional presence online, they are likely to be missing opportunities.

New Venues for Networking. Networking has always been a pillar of the job search process, providing candidates with access to the "unadvertised" job market and references to propel their candidacy for job opportunities. The changes and new directions of the typical job search, with employers' access to a seemingly limitless candidate pool online, heighten the importance of this skill. Not only is networking essential to the job search, but it is also a critical competency for professional success. A Collegiate Employment Research Institute survey of employers found that building and sustaining professional relationships was the most important skill for new college hires to demonstrate in their first professional position (Hanneman and Gardner, 2010). Networking skills are essential for success after college and practitioners have an important role to play in introducing students and graduates to new and emerging venues for networking. Such venues include social networking sites, which facilitate easier connections among students, alumni, and other professionals. Colleges and universities can serve as a catalyst for building those relationships, creating online alumni networks, as well as teaching students the tools and strategies to build their networks online. Offline, young professional organizations (YPOs) around the nation provide a venue for college graduates to connect and network within their communities. YPOs, whose membership typically includes those in their 20s and 30s, have cropped up around the country in communities seeking to attract and retain young workers. As such networking opportunities develop, they provide new opportunities that college graduates can access. In addition to teaching networking skills, savvy practitioners should introduce students to effective networking venues as they emerge.

Implications for Practitioners. As online communication and networking via social media and other venues gain prominence in the job search, practitioners can guide students to use these tools to their advantage. Because the media change so quickly, it is important to teach students the fundamentals of a professional online presence and networking rather than the technicalities of using any one specific website or tool. Pursuing knowledge about employer preferences with regard to electronic correspondence with candidates, format and style for uploaded application materials, and websites and forums for job openings equip student affairs practitioners to best advise students in their job search pursuits. Colleges and universities also play a role in establishing relationships among students, employers, alumni, and other professionals in their fields. Teaching networking skills, whether working a room or building online connections, is fundamental to job searches and professional success.

Specific practices may include employer panels advising students about online correspondence, seminars on keyword loading and other strategies to be found in an online search of resumes, virtual mock interviews using online media, and online image reviews to critique and advise students on developing their professional online presence. Networking events on campus, virtual job fairs, and alumni networking groups serve students well in their pursuit of professional contacts. Practitioners should teach both fundamentals of how to network and how to develop and maintain a professional reputation as well as how to apply those skills to various online or in-person media.

Changes in Higher Education and Job Preparedness

While the job market and recruiting practices have great influence on the preparation of students for after-college experiences, how job preparedness is defined warrants consideration. Certainly, employer expectations and hiring preferences help define what constitutes *workplace ready*. The influence of employers' preferences on higher education is mixed. Although some changes in higher education and curricula are made with an eye on job preparation, others are not. Whether or not they are motivated by the goal of preparing graduates for the workplace, all changes in higher education priorities and delivery influence the readiness of graduates for their professional lives. A review of changes in employer expectations and a sample of trends in higher education illustrate ways in which job preparedness is redefined by employers and influenced by higher education itself.

NEW DIRECTIONS FOR STUDENT SERVICES • DOI: 10.1002/ss

Escalation of Core Competency Expectations. Employer expectations of new professionals have long transcended technical competency in specific fields to include core professional skills that enable graduates to succeed in today's knowledge-based economy. Communication and teamwork abilities regularly top the list of skills employers seek, according to annual surveys conducted by the National Association of Colleges and Employers. However, studies indicate that while employers are generally satisfied that the majority of college graduates possess the skills necessary to succeed in entry-level positions, they are far less confident that graduates have the skills necessary for higher level jobs (Peter D. Hart Research Associates, 2008). Compounding the issue, Hanneman and Gardner (2010) argue that employers' expectations have increased over the last five years and that new graduates must demonstrate a level of ability and skill more traditionally associated with professionals in their second or third jobs. Their study shows that employers seek the same core professional skills, but at a higher level of competency than previously expected of new graduates. The skill escalation for new professionals results from sourcing out more routine job functions and demand for highly skilled professionals to fill gaps in the workforce once baby boomers retire (Hanneman and Gardner, 2010). The Association of American Colleges and Universities presses for cross-disciplinary training, rather than keeping students narrowly focused by major or department (2007). These changing demands for young professionals illustrate the need for college students to engage in challenging learning opportunities beyond their core curricula in order to prepare for their first jobs after college.

Internationalization. There is increasing discussion and focus among colleges and universities on internationalization, incorporating international elements in curricula, engaging international students and professors, and supporting travel, work, and study abroad by current students. However, there is mixed evidence of schools embracing internationalization as an institutional priority. While there is increasing support for students to study abroad and for faculty to pursue international experiences, less than half of the schools surveyed by the American Council on Education had full-time staff to oversee internationalization efforts and fewer yet with formal assessment of such efforts (Fischer, 2008). If internationalization trends take hold, they undoubtedly will influence students' preparation for work in a global economy. A study in 2009 by the International Association of Universities cited improving student preparedness as the number one priority for institutions promoting internationalization (Labi, 2009). As more students take advantage of opportunities to enhance their international knowledge and experience, it will be important for colleges and universities to help students showcase such experience as a selling point to potential employers.

Online and Accelerated Education. Two significant trends in higher education that may affect the preparation of students for careers and advanced studies include fast-growing enrollment in online learning opportunities and the concept of accelerated undergraduate degree programs. Online education has grown dramatically over the past decade. In 2007, the percentage growth of online enrollments was 9.7 in comparison to 1.5 percent growth in the overall higher education student population (Allen and Seaman, 2007). Institutions cite improved student access as the primary motivation for providing online learning opportunities (Allen and Seaman, 2007). Even among accredited programs, there is still concern about the quality of online education, especially in light of employers' high demand for communication, teamwork, and other critical professional competencies that may be a challenge to teach and practice in the virtual learning environment. However, initial skepticism of online learning may diminish as distance education grows in popularity and prevalence. A recent survey by the Society for Human Resource Management (SHRM) found that more than one third of organizations view an online degree as favorably as a traditional degree, and more than half reported that it would not make a difference in hiring decisions among candidates with similar experience for the job (2010).

A newer, but growing trend in undergraduate education is the concept of an accelerated degree program, such as a bachelor's degree in three years or associate's degree in one. The *Wall Street Journal* reports that in a 15-month period during 2009–2010, at least a dozen schools introduced new three-year accelerated bachelor's degree programs (Shellenbarger, 2010). Such degree plans enable students to complete the full credit requirements for a degree on a faster timeline by eliminating breaks and, in some programs, taking more courses per term. Programs may require students to declare a major earlier and leave less room for exploring other subjects through elective classes or extracurricular activities. Shellenbarger (2010) reports many state governments are encouraging, and some are even mandating, state universities to offer accelerated degree tracks. Accelerated programs demand focus, self-motivation, and time management. Some students value such programs as a fast track toward professional studies like law and medicine, saving time and money on an already long educational path of preparation (Shellenbarger, 2010). Although programs challenge students to declare majors early and offer little flexibility for changes, the rigor may enable students to quickly develop skills adaptable to the workplace and impress employers with their dedication. While there is a great deal of interest and momentum on the part of some related to the development of accelerated degree programs, there is also evidence that students are not among those embracing the movement (de Vise, 2011).

Dual enrollment in high school is another increasingly common avenue for pursuing accelerated education. Dual enrollment programs take several forms, all of which serve to allow upper-division high school students the opportunity to take courses that will count toward completion of both their high school diploma and a college degree. There is evidence to indicate that these programs are delivering, at least in part, on the expectations that proponents hold for them with regard to college participation and completion (Barnett and Stamm, 2010; Fleischman and Heppen, 2009; Karp, Calgano, Hughes, Jeon, and Bailey, 2007). Additional study is needed, however, to explore the ways in which accelerating the graduation of students from dual enrollment programs plays out in terms of their transition into graduate or professional school, military services, the workforce, or whatever their next step in life might be.

Implications for Practitioners. Job preparation may become a greater driver for changes in higher education as students become a blend of learner and consumer. A primary motivation for undergraduate students attending college is to get a good job. More than ever, prospective students and families evaluate undergraduate schools based on outcomes, considering graduate success rates and university support for career development. In 2007, the Princeton Review added career services to its ratings in response to these new demands. A good job might be the end goal for undergraduate students, but it's not always the focus for academic institutions. Academics have long debated college for the purpose of career preparation versus college for the purpose of learning, exploration, and enlightenment. Given the demands of constituents, both students and employers, higher education must balance both priorities. Interestingly, graduate students and programs reflect the perspective of traditional academe. Most graduate programs do not collect or publish job placement outcomes of graduates, nor do their prospective students seek it (Wilson, 2010). Practitioners should not only evaluate their own programs with an eye on job preparedness, but also educate their graduates to include career goals and outcomes in their graduate school decisions.

Employer demand for higher level competency in core professional skills creates a stronger need for schools to challenge students in new ways to help them develop the skills required to succeed in the workplace. Practitioners must consider the competency expectations of employers and how schools can improve flexibility of academic preparation by enhancing cross-disciplinary knowledge and skill development through course work, experiential learning, or programming with emphasis on skills needed for long-term career success.

Current trends in higher education must be evaluated in the light of job preparedness. Internationalization efforts enhance the effectiveness of graduates to compete in a global economy; however, students often need guidance in showcasing those experiences as professional strengths. Study abroad can advance students' skills in adaptability, problem solving, understanding different cultures and practices, and communicating effectively among various audiences. Practitioners can assist students in evaluation of their international experience to leverage it as a competitive advantage in the job search. Online learners present a creative challenge in development of core competencies since their virtual environment may limit experience in verbal communication or teamwork. Advancements in online class delivery make distance education a far more dynamic environment. However, practitioners can assist online learners in evaluating their skill levels and enhancing them with practical, real-world experience. Learners in accelerated programs may develop core competencies quickly or may find themselves lacking the skills desired by employers, without the extra time to develop and practice such skills. Careful advising and experiential learning will be critical for these students as well. Changes in higher education warrant preparation assistance designed to capitalize on the advantages of the system and overcome challenges.

Specific practices can include reentry sessions with students returning from study abroad, resume development highlighting international skills, and interview practice to communicate competencies built from international experience, as well as helping candidates with international expertise target employers and companies most likely to value such experience. For all students, reviews of employer expectations, as well as practical and curricular experience to develop and apply core competencies, are critical. Observations, business simulations, internships, and other experiential learning programs accelerate application of academic learning to practical environments. Collaboration with employers is essential. Partnerships between higher education and the business community integrate the expectations of employers with the training and preparation that postsecondary schools provide and contribute to the successful preparation of graduates even as both environments change.

Future Considerations

A review of current trends enables student affairs professionals and their colleagues to observe and project changes in their preparation of college graduates for their futures. However, there are certainly more questions for which there are not yet answers. Prevailing wisdom in the knowledge economy is that a college degree is pivotal in career advancement. To this end, initiatives like online education increase access to and availability of higher education. However, a segment of the workforce already has a higher level of education than necessary for the positions they hold. Will colleges and universities be overproducing graduates in the future? Will job creation remain relatively flat and result in underemployment? As the population's level of education increases, will a master's degree become as common a standard as the bachelor's degree is now?

Moreover, the changes in the job search process due to technology are dramatic. Will additional tools in virtual recruiting diminish the role of colleges and universities in the recruiting process? Given the trend of accelerated programs, will schools move from master's degree programs to postbaccalaureate or graduate certificates because they are shorter? Employer expectations are already rising. Will employers say that although institutions of higher education provide a good number of candidates, they are not high-quality graduates? Considering the emphasis placed by students and recent governmental efforts on outcomes of higher education, will institutions be held to a new level of accountability in terms of graduate success? As the job market, recruiting process, and higher education continue to evolve, student affairs professionals and their colleagues must recognize the trends, evaluate their impact on graduate success, and adjust their efforts to address new challenges and maximize opportunities for students in preparation for their lives after college.

References

Allen, I. E., and Seaman, J. "Online Nation: Five Years of Growth in Online Learning." *The Sloan Consortium.* Retrieved Oct. 17, 2010, from http://sloanconsortium.org /publications/survey/pdf/online_nation.pdf, 2007.

Association of American Colleges and Universities. "New Poll: Two-Thirds of Employers Say Graduates Lack Essential Skills." Retrieved July 18, 2011, from http://www .aacu.org/press_room/press_releases/2007/LEAPReport.cfm, 2007.

Barnett, E., and Stamm, L. "Dual Enrollment: A Strategy for Educational Advancement of All Students." Washington, DC: Blackboard Institute. Retrieved July 18, 2011, from http://www.blackboardinstitute.com/pdf/Bbinstitute_DualEnrollment.pdf, 2010.

Berman, J. "College Students Are Flocking to Sustainability Degrees, Careers." *USA Today,* August, 3, 2009. Retrieved May 17, 2011, from http://www.usatoday.com /news/education/2009-08-02-sustainability-degrees_N.htm.

Bureau of Labor Statistics, U.S. Department of Labor. "Selected Occupational Projections Data." Retrieved July 18, 2011, from http://data.bls.gov/oep/noeted, n.d.

Bureau of Labor Statistics, U.S. Department of Labor. *Career Guide to Industries, 2010– 2011 Edition, Healthcare.* Retrieved Aug. 4, 2010, from http://www.bls.gov/oco/cg /cgs035.htm, 2010a.

Bureau of Labor Statistics, U.S. Department of Labor. "Measuring Green Jobs." Retrieved Aug. 4, 2010, from http://www.bls.gov/green, 2010b.

Bureau of Labor Statistics, U.S. Department of Labor. "Occupational Employment." *Occupational Outlook Quarterly,* 53(4), 2010c.

BusinessWire. "Kaplan Test Prep and Admissions Survey: Parents More Involved in College Admissions Process, but Schools Philosophically Divided about How to Manage Them." *BusinessWire,* Sept. 27, 2010. Retrieved May 17, 2011, from http://www .businesswire.com/news/home/20100927005504/en/Kaplan-Test-Prep-Admissions-Survey-Parents-Involved.

Cohen, D. "Startups Replacing Summer Jobs." *Reuters,* June 23, 2010. Retrieved Oct. 9, 2010, from http://www.reuters.com/article/idUSTRE65M3A420100623.

Cross-Tab. "Online Reputation in a Connected World." Cross-Tab, January 2010. Retrieved Oct. 21, 2010, from http://www.microsoft.com/privacy/dpd/research.aspx.

de Vise, D. "3-Year College Degree Programs Not Catching On." *Washington Post,* June 15, 2011. Retrieved July 18, 2011, from http://www.washingtonpost.com /local/education/3-year-college-degree-programs-not-catching-on/2011/06/15 /AGX7VYWH_story.html.

Fischer, K. "New Report Reveals Mixed Results in Colleges' Efforts at International Education." *Chronicle of Higher Education,* May 30, 2008.

Fleischman, S., and Heppen, J. "Improving Low-Performing High Schools: Searching for Evidence of Promise." *America's High Schools,* 19(1). Retrieved July 18, 2011, from http://www.princeton.edu/futureofchildren/publications/journals/article/index.xml? journalid=30&articleid=50&sectionid=186, 2009.

Hanneman, L., and Gardner, P. (2010, February). "Under the Economic Turmoil a Skills Gap Simmers." Lansing, MI: Collegiate Employment Research Institute, Michigan State University. Retrieved Apr. 20, 2010, from http://www.ceri.msu.edu/wp-content /uploads/2010/01/skillsabrief1-2010.pdf, 2010.

Howe, N., and Strauss, W. (2007). *Millennials Go to College: Strategies for a New Generation on Campus* (2nd ed.). Washington, DC: American Association of College Registrars, 2007.

Jobvite. "Social Recruiting Survey." Burlingame, CA: Jobvite. Retrieved Oct.21, 2010, from http://recruiting.jobvite.com/resources/social-recruiting-survey.php, 2010.

Karp, M. M., Calgano, J. C., Hughes, K. L., Jeong, D. W., and Bailey, T. R. "The Postsecondary Achievement of Participants in Dual Enrollment: An Analysis of Student Outcomes in Two States." New York: Community College Research Center, Teachers College, Columbia University. Retrieved July 18, 2011, from http://136.165.122.102 /UserFiles/File/pubs/Dual_Enrollment.pdf, 2007.

Katel, P. "Jobs Outlook: Is a College Education Important?" *CQ Researcher*, 20(21), 2010.

Kauffman Foundation. (2010). "Despite Recession, U.S. Entrepreneurial Activity Rises in 2009 to Highest Rate in 14 Years, Kauffman Study Shows." Kansas City, MO: Kauffman Foundation. Retrieved Oct. 9, 2010, from http://www.kauffman.org/newsroom /despite-recession-us-entrepreneurial-activity-rate-rises-in-2009.aspx, 2010.

Labi, A. "Priorities in Internationalization Shift from Research to Preparing Students." *Chronicle of Higher Education*, Sept. 20, 2009. Retrieved Dec. 11, 2010, from http:// chronicle.com/article/Internationalizations-Focus/48530.

Madden, K. "New Generation of Entrepreneurs." *CNN.com*, Oct. 9, 2010. Retrieved Oct. 9, 2010, from http://articles.cnn.com/2010-08-11/living/cb.new.entrepreneurs _1_job-market-teaching-entrepreneurs-young-people?s=PM:LIVING.

National Association of Colleges and Employers. "Looking Ahead: Highlights from the Future Trends Survey." *NACE Journal*, LXX(1), 2009.

Peter D. Hart Research Associates. "How Should Colleges Assess and Improve Student Learning?" Peter D. Hart Research Associates, 2008. Retrieved Apr. 20, 2010, from http://www.aacu.org/leap/documents/2008_Business_Leader_Poll.pdf, 2008.

Pew Charitable Trusts. "The Clean Energy Economy: Repowering Jobs, Businesses, and Investments across America." Pew Charitable Trusts, 2009. Retrieved Aug. 4, 2010, from http://www.pewcenteronthestates.org/uploadedFiles/Clean_Economy_Report _Web.pdf, 2009.

Pew Internet and American Life Project. "Reputation Management and Social Media: How People Monitor Their Identity and Search for Others Online." Pew Internet and American Life Project, 2010. Retrieved Oct. 21, 2010, from http://www.pewinternet .org/Press-Releases/2010/Reputation-Management.aspx, 2010.

Shellenbarger, S. "Speeding College to Save $10,000." *The Wall Street Journal*, May 12, 2010. Retrieved May 25, 2010, from http://online.wsj.com/article/SB1000142405274 8703565804575238341696523742.html.

Society of Human Resources Management. "SHRM Poll: Hiring Practices and Attitudes: Traditional vs. Online Degree Credentials." Alexandria, VA: Society of Human Resources Management, Aug. 2010. Retrieved Oct. 17, 2010, from http://www.shrm .org/Research/SurveyFindings/Articles/Pages/HiringPracticesandAttitudes.aspx.

Wilson, R. "The Quality Measure That Graduate Schools Shun." *The Chronicle of Higher Education*, Nov. 28, 2010. Retrieved May 17, 2011, from http://chronicle.com/article /The-Quality-Measure-That/125544/.

ELIZABETH J. BUSHNELL is the director of Career Services at Manchester College.

INDEX

Accelerated education, 98–100

ACPA. *See* American College Personnel Association (ACPA)

ACPA/NASPA task force. *See* American College Personnel Association and National Association of Student Personnel Administrators

After-college life, pathway programs to, 29–40; for community college to university transition, 31–33; and defining programming, 30; future of, 39–40; theories and models of, 29–30; and types of transitions and programming to support students, 30–31; for undergraduate to graduate studies transition, 33–34; for university to military transition, 37–39; for university to work transition, 34–37

After-college life, preparation for, 5–11; and accountability, 7; and building relationships, disappearing borders, 10; contemporary context of, 6–10; and economic conditions, 9–10; and family involvement, 7; historical context of, 5–6; and learning, 7–8; and student demographics, 8–9

Alcott, L. M., 29

Allen, I. E., 91, 99

Allentown College. *See* DeSales University

Alsop, R., 8

American Association of Community Colleges, 31

American College Personnel Association (ACPA), 7–8, 10

American College Personnel Association and National Association of Student Personnel Administrators task force (ACPA/NASPA task force), 10

American Physical Therapy Association (APTA), 68

Anticipatory socialization, 15

APTA. *See* American Physical Therapy Association (APTA)

Articulation agreements, 59–62

Associated Press, 32

Association of American Colleges and Universities, 98

Astin, A. W., 19

Author of one's life phase, becoming (self-authorship), 16

Bailey, T. R., 100

Bakersfield College (California), 60

Barnett, E., 100

Barr, M. J., 30

Barry University (Miami Shores, Florida), 43, 56; Adrian Dominican School of Education, 43; College of Arts and Sciences, 43; College of Health Sciences, 43; Dwayne O. Andreas School of Law, 43; Ellen Whiteside McDonnell School of Social Work, 43; Graduate School Awareness Week, 43–46; Graduate School Information Fair, 44; School of Human Performance and Leisure Sciences, 43; School of Podiatric Medicine, 43

Berman, J., 93

Bickel, R. D., 7

Blackmer, B., 68, 69

BLS. *See* United States Bureau of Labor Statistics (BLS)

Blustein, D. L., 9, 11, 23, 24

Bohling, A. J., 9, 11, 23, 24

Boomer generation, 22

Burack, C., 10

Bushnell, E. J., 91

BusinessWire, 95

Calgano, J. C., 100

Capstone courses, 71

Career Academy (University of Georgia, Athens), 50–53; budget and responsibility for, 51–52; idea for, 50–51; program, 51; program goals and assessment for, 52–53; sample schedule for, 52

Career courses: and four-year colleges and universities, 64; and general career courses, 66–67; and graduate and professional programs to work, 68–69; impact and availability of, 63–64; and learning outcomes, 64–66; major-specific, 67; prevalence of, 62–63; and transition to graduate education, 69–71; and transition to work, 68; and two-year colleges, 64; variation in design of, 66

NEW DIRECTIONS FOR STUDENT SERVICES

ORDER FORM SUBSCRIPTION AND SINGLE ISSUES

DISCOUNTED BACK ISSUES:

Use this form to receive 20% off all back issues of *New Directions for Student Services*.
All single issues priced at **$23.20** (normally $29.00)

TITLE	ISSUE NO.	ISBN
_____	_____	_____
_____	_____	_____
_____	_____	_____

Call 888-378-2537 or see mailing instructions below. When calling, mention the promotional code JBNND to receive your discount. For a complete list of issues, please visit www.josseybass.com/go/ndss

SUBSCRIPTIONS: (1 YEAR, 4 ISSUES)

☐ New Order   ☐ Renewal

U.S.	☐ Individual: $89	☐ Institutional: $275
CANADA/MEXICO	☐ Individual: $89	☐ Institutional: $315
ALL OTHERS	☐ Individual: $113	☐ Institutional: $349

Call 888-378-2537 or see mailing and pricing instructions below.
Online subscriptions are available at www.onlinelibrary.wiley.com

ORDER TOTALS:

Issue / Subscription Amount: $ _____

Shipping Amount: $ _____
(for single issues only – subscription prices include shipping)

Total Amount: $ _____

SHIPPING CHARGES:
First Item $6.00
Each Add'l Item $2.00

(No sales tax for U.S. subscriptions. Canadian residents, add GST for subscription orders. Individual rate subscriptions must be paid by personal check or credit card. Individual rate subscriptions may not be resold as library copies.)

BILLING & SHIPPING INFORMATION:

☐ **PAYMENT ENCLOSED:** *(U.S. check or money order only. All payments must be in U.S. dollars.)*

☐ **CREDIT CARD:**   ☐ VISA   ☐ MC   ☐ AMEX

Card number _____ Exp. Date_____

Card Holder Name_____ Card Issue # _____

Signature _____ Day Phone_____

☐ **BILL ME:** *(U.S. institutional orders only. Purchase order required.)*

Purchase order # _____
Federal Tax ID 13559302 • GST 89102-8052

Name_____

Address_____

Phone_____ E-mail_____

Copy or detach page and send to: **John Wiley & Sons, One Montgomery Street, Suite 1200,**
San Francisco, CA 94104-4594

Order Form can also be faxed to: **888-481-2665**

PROMO JBNND